R08333

BOOK NUMBER

WITHDRAWN
FROM STOCK

D1610365

BATTLE FOR THE HIGH STREET

381.0941
KAY

William Kay

BATTLE FOR THE HIGH STREET

PIATKUS

ACKNOWLEDGEMENTS

I should like to thank all the companies mentioned in this book for the invaluable time and help they gave me. Without them it would not have been possible to find out their latest thinking on what has been, and promises to be, one of Britain's most changeable industries.

Quite properly, however, the companies' directors and spokespeople had a view of their own firms. The retail team at Wood Mackenzie, the stockbrokers, provided me with a valuable source of counterbalance by giving me access to their research work.

Finally, this book would not have happened without the prompting, persistence and patience of Gill Cormode and Judy Piatkus of Piatkus Books. Nonetheless, all opinions and errors are my very own.

William Kay
London, 1987

© 1987 William Kay

First published in 1987 by
Judy Piatkus (Publishers) Limited,
5 Windmill Street, London W1P 1HF

British Library Cataloguing in Publication Data
Kay, William
    Battle for the high street.
    1. Retail trade
    I. Title
    658.8'7   HF5429
    ISBN 0-86188-621-6

Designed by Paul Saunders
Phototypeset in 11/13pt Baskerville by
D.P. Media Limited, Hitchin, Hertfordshire
Printed and bound in Great Britain by
Mackays of Chatham Ltd.

Contents

The High Street Revolution

A revolution is sweeping through Britain's high streets. Greater spending power and more leisure time are restoring the customer to a position he or she has not known since before the Second World War. The retailer is now dancing to the public's tune, rather than the other way around. But, as new shopping ideas tumble out on to the streets at an ever more hectic rate, retailers appear less and less certain what that tune is.

Each new style captures the imagination for a few months or years before it is overtaken by another. We seem to have entered an era of disposable shops, reshaped and redecorated in an effort to match changes in the public's mood, while even the most established high street chains endeavour to combat the constant threat of losing their customers.

'Chain stores have been the most difficult part of our business' said Desmond Pitcher, chief executive of Littlewoods, which also runs mail order and football pools. 'We rode on the crest of the wave like everybody else in the 1970s, but when the competition came in the 1980s we had to try to find our identity. Our biggest single problem has been getting more people over the doorstep.'

Littlewoods, like Marks & Spencer and John Lewis, has had to adapt in an effort to defend its share of the market. For the newer and more innovative groups intent on attacking that market, design has been the watchword, whether of the goods on the shelves or the shops themselves. Men like Rodney Fitch, Michael Page and Stewart McColl have become millionaires on the back of their ability to brighten up the dullest store. They would concede that they owe much to Sir Terence Conran for making retailers more design-conscious. Conran can claim credit for fostering the revolution both as a designer and as the driving force behind Habitat, Mothercare, Heal's and BhS.

Before the war, service was the key to successful selling. Wages were low, hours were long, and manufacturers' insistence on a system of Resale Price Maintenance made it hard for shops to compete by cutting prices. But the war's restrictions tilted the balance of power away from the consumer. The need to save energy meant that corner shops closed at 6 pm instead of midnight, while shortages made shoppers grateful for whatever shopkeepers could supply. Post-war rationing continued to give the retailer the upper hand until 1954 and beyond, for even after rationing was removed fifteen years of restrictions had brainwashed many British shoppers into taking whatever the high street felt like selling them.

Today's revolution is the latest battle in the David and Goliath struggle which has been taking place since the last century between the independent shopkeeper and the big battalions of department stores and multiple chains.

That hundred years' war was sparked off by, of all things, the Great Exhibition, a celebration of the best of British work and craftsmanship displayed in the mighty Crystal Palace in Hyde Park in 1851. The sight of so many goods under one roof inspired William Whiteley to build Britain's first department store a mile or so away in Bayswater in 1863. One or two large clothing stores had been departmentalised by then, notably Manchester's Kendal Milne and Bainbridge's of Newcastle, but Whiteley's was the first to try to offer a wide range of goods under one roof.

Battle was joined, as it has been ever since, between the competing claims of the store that has everything and the personal service of the local shop that depends on its particular speciality for its proprietor's livelihood. The showmanship which went with the desire to open a department store combined with the architectural possibilities of such large buildings to produce striking, eye-catching interiors which made shopping in them an event and appealed to the middle classes, at whom they were principally aimed.

But the turnover the department stores needed to pay for themselves ensured that none but the largest towns could support more than one or two apiece. Unless a shopper was determined on making an expedition, the local shops were still more convenient and were all most people could afford. In those days most of them tended to sell food of one sort or another, which is bulky to carry home without either a good transport service or – an unimaginable rarity in those days – a private car. So the independent shops reinforced their advantage by delivering goods to their best customers' homes.

The next blow against the independents was the advent of the multiple chains. One of the first of these was the Co-operative Movement, an unconventional organisation which was a difficult target for local shopkeepers as it was technically owned by the local community – the very people whose custom they were competing for. It grew rapidly and was soon big enough to argue for bulk discounts from suppliers, whilst passing the benefit on to the owners/customers in the form of a dividend.

Entrepreneurs behind firms like Lipton's, Boots and W H Smith soon saw that if they could create their own multiple chains they could have the same bulk-buying power and give the personal service of their local rivals, yet keep the extra profit for themselves. And people travelling away from their own town would be more likely to patronise a shop that had a name and style they were familiar with. This was an easier target to rail against, and the independents unsuccessfully complained that the multiples amounted to unfair competition. Wholesalers were none too pleased either, because they found themselves getting cut out by multiples intent on buying direct from manufacturers.

One or two American groups like Woolworth had seen that there were opportunities for the taking in the UK high street. They promoted the idea of persuading suppliers to prepack goods under well-advertised brand names instead of delivering them in bulk for the shopkeeper to carve up or ladle out. That added to the buying power of the big chains, but it helped the smaller retailers too, because they did not need to spend as much time on training new recruits in the art of handling and repacking merchandise and could take on school leavers who were less intelligent and therefore cheaper.

But the next major onslaught on the corner shop came in the late 1940s, when Britain was still in the grip of post-war austerity. The grocery chains decided to save even more money on staff by importing the self-service idea from America. Supermarkets had arrived.

Although they were eventually to be the death-knell of many a local grocer, the British public's initial response to supermarkets was not enthusiastic. Some were embarrassed because the wire baskets exposed to everyone's gaze how little they might be buying. Others resented the lack of a chat with the salesgirl. A few felt that as customers it was not their job to be taking goods off the shelves and carrying them round the shop. And in one legendary case a woman threw a basket at the future Lord Sainsbury to record her protest at the new barbarism!

But people grew to like helping themselves, particularly if they had not got on with the assistant who had stood between them and their groceries under the old regime. Lower prices, usually plastered across the windows of the supermarkets, were enough to overcome most people's misgivings. As the Co-op found to its cost, shoppers eventually decided they preferred lower prices to any of the frills, including dividends.

The 1950s and 1960s saw the beginnings of social trends that were to make an indelible impact on the retailing scene. The 1950s are seen now as years of rebellion, characterised by teddy boys and rock 'n' roll – another American import. Theories abound to explain why this happened. Soldiers, the nucleus of the immediate post-war crop of parents, even before they returned from the front elected a Labour government which would put an end to the old order and bring equality to all. The Conservatives responded to this with an even more bewitching promise – that living standards would double within 25 years.

To bring that about, the factories began humming in the 1950s. They produced more goods than ever before at prices within everyone's reach. Cars, electrical goods and furniture spilled into the showrooms. There was also a significant rise in trade union membership, as the workers in those factories sought to ensure that they got their share of the new wealth.

More of that money filtered into the hands of the young, first through the wages they were paid and then through the pocket money their younger brothers and sisters received from their parents. Teenagers were identified as an economic force, because of the spending power they were acquiring. They were not inclined just to accept what they were given, but wanted new clothes, make-up and pop records, and quickly. Independent television was launched in Britain in 1955, bringing a powerful new form of consumer advertising into the home. Cinema attendances soared, giving advertisers another chance to reach the young.

The new generation of consumers was paralleled by a new generation of retailers and manufacturers who were making themselves felt, people who might have been born before the war but were only children when peace broke out. In 1955 Mary Quant caused a sensation when she opened the first branch of Bazaar in London's King's Road. Shoppers queued to get in. That sensation may at first have been confined to fashionable London, but its ripples gradually spread out across the country. The public realised that shops and shopping could be fun, that they did not have to be confined to the traditional straitjacket.

13

That mood led Sir Terence Conran from being a furniture manufacturer to becoming a retailer. He was unhappy with the way the old-style furniture stores displayed his goods. He opened his first Habitat in 1964. 'We were convinced that there was a gap in the market. We just started one shop to show how we would like it done. We already had a showroom, and this was just an extension of that as far as we could see. But having started, we discovered a whole new world. Other retailers told us it would never work outside Chelsea, so we opened our third store in Manchester to see who was right. As it happened we were, and things just went on from there.'

Just as Habitat was born out of a manufacturer's desire to see his goods displayed properly, so some retailers began to use their buying power to insist on stricter standards from their suppliers. Marks & Spencer led the way in laying down detailed specifications for its manufacturers, some of whom relied on M & S to take as much as ninety per cent of their output. MFI, the discount furniture chain, was another to state exactly what it wanted for the price it was willing to pay, based in turn on the price it felt it could charge.

It was no coincidence that from these seeds the 1960s also saw the emergence of consumerism as a political force. The abolition of Resale Price Maintenance in 1964 meant that retailers were free to make their own minds up about the prices they would set, with the exception of a few items such as books and newspapers. The 1968 Trades Descriptions Act controlled the claims that manufacturers could make about their products.

The end of RPM was a severe blow to the small shopkeeper. Although it was hailed as a triumph for the consumer, the spadework had been carried out by the up-and-coming supermarket groups. In an echo of the more recent campaign to liberalise Sunday trading, supermarkets had been ignoring RPM and daring suppliers to sue. As far back as 1955 the retailers had been given the court's backing to continue their fight: the change in the law nine years later did little more than recognise the fact that a determined retailer could cut prices at will. Discounting spread from food to electrical appliances and other consumer durables, and the smaller retailers found that they were buying from the wholesaler at the same price their aggressive rivals were charging the customer.

The business of creating and placing advertisements became vitally important if a manufacturer was to be heard in this cacophony. Working in an advertising agency became one of the fashionable things to do in the 1960s. It was making use of what then seemed to be almost magical new marketing and research techniques – again largely imported from America at that stage – which claimed to offer the client the ability to target and control the consumer to a degree previously unheard of. It also gave scope for the personal creativity that had become so desirable at that time. Advertising soon attracted people even younger than the new breed of retailers, who were shrewdly recruited by the agency bosses for their ability to talk to their own generation.

This amounted to more dismal news for the independent shop-keeper. The emphasis on price-cutting, combined with the growing advertising overhead, gave manufacturers a strong incentive to push their goods through the multiples and the supermarkets, where the volume sales lay.

New retailers could still break into the market, but only if they saw a clear gap and had the vision and determination to exploit it. What made shops like Habitat, Mothercare and Laura Ashley different from their predecessors was that they were above all ideas merchants. They were selling their customers a concept, a lifestyle, a fresh way of looking at furniture or baby clothes or women's fashions.

The translation of these concepts into established chains made others realise that this could be an important signpost to the future. People have to want to go into a shop, particularly if it is selling something as personal as clothes or furniture, and they prefer to go into a shop that their friends agree is one of the shops to be seen in. A phenomenon of the past twenty years has been the branded carrier bag, so that customers of a particular shop can let everyone else know where they go shopping.

Not that all these brave new ideas succeeded. Perhaps the apotheosis of the 'themed' store was Biba, a fashion shop which started in a small way in the Kensington district of London and in 1974 took over the old Derry and Toms department store in Kensington High Street. It was supposed to be an experience: there was no pressure to buy, and the store even provided comfortable armchairs for customers to relax in. The turnover was not enough to pay the rent, and pilfering reached record heights.

A large number of independent retailers were coming under intense pressure without making mistakes like that, simply from the strength of competition. This was at its strongest in groceries, where there is less scope for the small man to hit back through innovation and Asda, J. Sainsbury and Tesco were reinforcing their bulk-buying power by marketing goods aggressively under their own label. As more and more people acquired their own cars, the supermarket groups began to provide parking at the back so that shoppers had every incentive to buy a week's shopping in one trip, leaving the corner shop with little more than the few crumbs to be had from meeting small emergency purchases.

The 1970s saw a further polarisation of the high street. Indeed, the big stores began to burst out of the high street and into fields on the edge of town. They took the idea from IKEA of Sweden, who discovered that people liked their cars so much that they would happily use the excuse to drive to a warehouse fifteen miles away if there was a wide range of choice and the chance of a bargain. MFI, Texas Homecare, Woolco and the inevitable supermarkets snapped up cheap land with plenty of parking. Shopping centres soon followed. The all-weather pedestrian precinct was exported out of town, where shoppers could find all their favourite stores under one roof.

That might have left the high street deserted. But, by and large, it did not. President Idi Amin made a major contribution to the reinvigoration of the British shopping scene by expelling thousands of Ugandan Asians, many of whom came to England with nothing but their skill as shopkeepers – and their willingness to stay open as long as there were customers. Many of them took advantage of the help available to redesign the traditional confectionery, tobacconist and newsagent shops on the latest lines, with floor-to-ceiling rows of magazines along one wall and tempting racks of sweets near the till. That help came, understandably enough, from magazine publishers like IPC who were concerned to revive flagging sales.

The high street was becoming the stamping ground for the impulse purchase and the emergency service, as well as the more leisurely stroll to make comparisons. It always had met these needs, and clothes shops have survived because of the desire to pick and choose. The bank, the chemist, the pub and the fish-and-chip shop still cater for casual and local needs. But now the gaps in the high street were being filled by building societies, estate agents, wine bars and takeaway food covering anything from hamburgers to Peking duck.

But the history of British retailing has been regularly punctuated by examples of the big groups' ability to jump on a bandwagon. The new-style corner shop was no exception, once it had been established that what people really wanted from their local store was the convenience of being able to pop into it at any hour of the evening, just like in the old days.

In a sense, the Ugandan Asians had reintroduced a concept, which new chains like Eight Till Late and 7-Eleven proceeded to refine into a form that could be repeated. What they had noticed was that consumers were less price-conscious when they shopped early or late. They appeared to accept that convenience stores were entitled to charge for the extra service they were providing. If that could be married to bulk buying from head office, there was room to give the shop manager strong incentive payments in return for his unsocial hours.

However, that was no more than the local shops had had to get used to every so often for years past as their bigger rivals tried to muscle in on the latest new idea. For more than a decade a much more menacing threat had been gathering: Sunday trading.

It is now a matter of history that in April 1986 a combination of disaffected Ulster Unionist MPs and a Conservative backbench rebellion killed a Government Bill to liberalise shopping on Sunday. But the heat and emotion generated by that issue revealed more about the British public's deeply divided attitudes towards the sort of retailing service they really wanted than ever before. To a degree we all want to have our cake and eat it: the best goods at the lowest price from the big chains, and a few shops within walking distance to cater for the odd emergency. The march of the multiples had cast a veil over the affection with which millions of consumers regarded their corner shops. That veil was suddenly lifted.

Everyone seemed to agree that the existing law was a nonsense. The 1950 Shops Act had thrown up such a lengthy list of glaring anomalies that it had fallen into abuse. It permitted newspapers and magazines, however lurid, to be sold on Sundays, but not Bibles or any other books or records – to the considerable embarrassment of the churches, some of which had been doing just that even though they were opposed to the proposed new legislation.

The Lord's Day Observance Society had fought a spirited campaign against reform, but over the years had been beaten back on several counts. It was ironic that a bastion of conservatism, the cricket establishment, had found a way round the strictures against professional sport on Sunday as long ago as 1967. Football cautiously followed.

But perhaps the most significant breach in the tradition was made by the decision of big retailers to open on Good Friday, which had previously been as sacrosanct as Christmas Day. Employees were willing to serve, lured by generous overtime rates and an extra day off, and more than enough customers seemed glad of the chance to go somewhere on what they regarded as an otherwise barren day. The habit soon caught on and spread to other holidays, and thence to Sunday itself. Meanwhile the law was amended separately in Scotland and was working well. God-fearing souls north of the Border boasted about how they did their shopping in the morning and went to Church in the evening.

In England and Wales, anomalies between what goods could and could not be legally sold were compounded by the different degrees to which the law was enforced round the country. It was up to local councils to prosecute offending shops. Some pursued their quarry to the very letter of the law, while others turned a blind eye. In any case, the retailers were still comfortably in profit even after paying fines.

It was no surprise that the free-market Thatcher Government took it upon itself to bring the law up to date. It had all the signs of being a popular reform, especially in the run-up to a general election. It would also be an excellent curtain-raiser for plans to extend public house hours.

But then the die-hards began to show their teeth, and the corner-shop side of the British character emerged. The Union of Shop, Distributive and Allied Workers predictably sprang to its members' defence. Church leaders drew up petitions of parishioners who preferred Sunday as it was. A cunning campaign developed around the slogan 'Keep Sunday Special'.

Even that would not have been quite enough, had the Ulster Unionists not decided to abandon their boycott of Westminster in the hope of doing the Government down. It was, though, enough to put the wind up nearly 50 Tory MPs, many of whom had been receiving torrents of mail against the Bill and were suffering drubbings at public meetings on the subject. They either abstained or voted against the Bill.

The high street has in fact turned into a series of battles as the various groups try to dominate or fight off their nearest rivals. The succeeding chapters try to highlight the main issues in each of those battles, and then take a closer look at two or three of the main protagonists. Judge for yourself who is likely to end up on top.

The Iron Fist in the Designer Glove

THE PROTAGONISTS:
- *STOREHOUSE*
- *NEXT*

Design is one of the retailing watchwords of the 1980s, spawning several millionaires in its own right and transforming the appearance of the high street. Shops and their frontages have always had to be designed, of course. They do not just happen by accident. As a deliberate means of creating a mood and attracting a certain range of customers, shop design began to come into its own on May 11, 1964, when the 33-year-old Terence Conran opened his first branch of Habitat in Fulham, west London. Habitat has since become and remained a byword for high-street chic. But, in the ever-competitive world of retailing, others soon picked up the message that with the help of clever design they could corner a clientele and encourage them to spend more often within the framework of a distinctive look that reflected their personal aspirations towards a particular lifestyle.

It is not surprising that the favourite target of this type of approach has been the 20-30 age group, with plenty of money in their pockets and a need to show that they are aware of the latest trends. The 1960s was the decade when fashionable boutiques sprang up, followed within a few years by the first of Laura Ashley's individualistic women's clothing shops. At about this time Conran's separate design consultancy ventured into the mass market when it put together the basic theme of the Top Shop chain.

That was an early example of co-operation between Conran and Ralph Halpern, then an up-and-coming executive in the buying department of the Burton Group, Top Shop's parent. It also brought to the fore Rodney Fitch, a Conran employee who went on to break away and form his own company, now Fitch & Co. Design Consultants, which has become one of the pacemakers in this new industry. He has since taken his drawing pad to Boots, Woolworth, Wimpy, the main Burton chain and Heathrow's Terminal Four.

'Consumers' ideas, expectations and attitudes towards retailing, towards how they will buy, let alone what they will buy – and the centrally changing position of the woman's role – are all in a state of flux,' said Fitch. 'High street shopping simply mirrors changes in our society, and one of the main changes is an increased expectation of quality. Retailing is possibly the most competitive business there is, and to be successful you have to demonstrate that you are responsive to these changes. Design has become a part of these competitive retail strategies. Design is a visual thing, and therefore the end result is a visual change.'

But it was not until Habitat had become an established success that the competition began to analyse design's role in the complex mixture which makes a winning retail formula. Price was becoming less important than quality, but it had to be a quality wanted by a definable audience in sufficient numbers. So design inevitably led backwards into market segmentation, subsequently refined into the concepts of theming, focusing and selling retail stories. They all stemmed from the realisation that the retailer had a weapon which gave him the power to influence, seduce and even manipulate the customer into buying in a pattern and with a frequency which best suited the retail operation. It was every bit as important as the advertising campaign, and indeed went hand in hand with it.

Although the impact of design has made itself felt even in such traditionally price-dominated areas as supermarkets, its power is strongest in shops catering for impulse purchases, wants rather than needs, and where the look of the goods matters as much as their ability to do the job. In high street terms, that means clothing, household goods and personal care products. Of these, clothing and household goods have received most of the attention as the average price is higher than most people are willing to pay for toiletries or perfumes on a regular basis.

Fashion has also proved to be one of the mainstays of the high street. It has resisted the drift of out-of-town locations, with the exception of shopping centres such as Brent Cross in north London or the Metro Centre in Gateshead, which are really high streets by another name. Comparison is important to fashion shoppers, as is the notion of the unpremeditated lunchtime stroll down the street, in case there is something new to catch the eye. Although shopping centres demand a deliberate journey, once there the customer can turn the trip into the same sort of strolling approach.

In the early days of the design revolution the incoming commercial groups, as opposed to the innovators, saw design as little more than an excuse for a shouting match. Loudest was best. But now cool is cooler, thanks to the success of groups like Benetton, the Italian sweater and jeans company which operates a form of international franchise operation. The shopkeepers do not pay a royalty on turnover, as regular franchisees do, but they must fit out their shops to precise specifications and stock only Benetton goods.

Meanwhile Conran has propagated his urbane version of good taste beyond Habitat into Mothercare, Heal's, Richards and BhS through a series of friendly takeovers which have taken him into every major high street in the land and quite a few overseas. While many others recognise the value of design, the company which comes closest to Conran in terms of its determination to dictate a particular style is Next, which began in clothes and has moved into furnishings under its aggressive boss, George Davies.

The rivalry is understandable, given that Conran was a director and then chairman of Next when it was called J. Hepworth & Son, and Davies came into the group with the concept that provided the germ for Next. Conran presided over the launch of Next as a chain of shops selling women's co-ordinates, but resigned in 1983 to avoid a conflict of interest with a new project he had in mind for Habitat, a teens' chain under the Now banner. Ironically, Now never captured the imagination of its target audience and was wound down three years later. Meanwhile Conran's company bought Richards, which put him into the mainstream of fashion retailing. Had he stayed at Next, it is conceivable that he could have merged it into the rest of his retailing operations. Instead, he and Davies snap at one another's heels, which is not bad thing as far as the consumer is concerned.

The designers seem to have organised themselves a job for life. The logic of theme shops points to narrower and narrower targeting, limited only by the minimum rate of sales to make a shop profitable. And the target never stands still, least of all in the fashion trade, implying that the most competitive chains are going to have to change their look more and more frequently. Next seems to be turning itself into something resembling the genus that inhabits the film Aliens, spawning and splitting itself into ever more variations. 'We were in danger of losing our exclusivity,' said Davies – and the design teams doubtless rubbed their hands at the thought of another set of fees.

Some heretical voices are beginning to be heard casting doubts on the designer high street. Woolworth Holdings and W H Smith are two of the groups whose senior directors have pointed to the cost of refurbishing an entire chain to bring its colours and look up to date. They speak with feeling, as both companies have recently done just that. And of course it has to be done from time to time, just to keep the shops looking presentable. Peeling paint and threadbare carpet are less than appealing. No, the question is how often can a chain afford to smarten itself? Smith operates on an eight-year cycle. Some of the more fashion-oriented retailers seem to be heading down towards a four-year spell between new looks.

That, say the sceptics, is all very well when there is a consumer boom to pay for it. What happens when that boom tails off, as it eventually must? The answer may be to throw some of the problem back at the designers by asking them to accept instalment payments, or even payment by results. The alternative is ever so gently to extend the refit cycle, hoping customers will not notice. But fashion is a particularly competitive trade which relies almost entirely upon look. If one chain reaches for the paintbrush, the others must think seriously about following suit or risk being deafened by the click of passers-by heels as they march on to the spruced-up rival. In a shrinking market, which is hard to imagine after the last few years but cannot be far away, that will put pressure on the laggards to keep spending or be left behind.

Consciously innovative and thoughtful may have become a necessary adjunct to modern lifestyles; it could also turn into a treadmill for the retailer who is not fully committed to it as business lifestyle.

THE CONRAN EMPIRE

Sir Terence Conran, who began his business life as a furniture maker in a Bethnal Green workshop more than thirty years ago, has latterly collected under his wing some of the top names in the British high street. Having created and established Habitat as one of the retail success stories of the 1960s and 1970s, he has spent much of the 1980s picking up chains that were running out of steam and needed an injection of his special brand of magic. Mothercare, Heal's, Richards and BhS have been brought together with Habitat and the US-based Conran's under the name of Storehouse, a label which is used not on the high street but only on the Stock Exchange for the purpose of identifying these diverse interests under one investment umbrella. Such a powerful collection means that Sir Terence, knighted in 1983, has moved effortlessly from being regarded as an idiosyncratic guru of high street design to one of the mainstream leaders of the retail sector. Yet, comfortably ensconced in his fifties, he manages to retain the sense of fun of a small boy who has just written his first computer program . . . and it works!

'Retailing was a very dull business in the old days,' he recalled. 'Shops were really just warehouses for exchanging goods for money, and design was supposed to be only for the middle classes. There was an arrogance about retailers that a certain grade of product was "good enough" for the masses.'

When Conran left Bryanston School he studied textile design at the Central School of Art and Design. His first real chance to cut his teeth on a public project was at the Festival of Britain in 1951, where he designed furniture and fabrics for the Homes and Gardens exhibition.

'At the end of the war there was a tremendous pent-up demand for goods,' he said. 'But the Festival of Britain had no influence at all, and that puzzled me for some time. I decided the reason was that because anybody could sell anything they made, why should you as a factory go and do new things and take risks? So the effect did not work its way through to the shops.'

Conran was busily doing new things and taking risks, and still finding it hard to break through. He made furniture at his Bethnal Green outpost, then hopped on the underground and took it to the West End stores. In between times he did some freelance design work for manufacturers. He dabbled in snack bars, opened a restaurant in King's Road and imported basketware from Madeira.

But in the 1950s he was also beginning to realise that something was seriously amiss about the way most goods, and especially furniture, were being presented on the high street.

Conran explained: 'When I started there were a lot of people coming out of art school who were frustrated with the great constipated turd of retailing, people like Mary Quant and Barbara Hulanicki. The same was true of the restaurant business.

There was a feeling that the "golden age of shoddy merchandise" had ended.' Quant created a sensation in 1955 when she opened the first branch of Bazaar, her fashion chain. Conran caught the mood by designing another branch for her two years later. The success of Bazaar made him realise that the shop is as important a part of the product as the product itself.

On holidays in France he could not help noticing how shoppers responded to the informality of being able to buy furniture directly from workshops, where the goods were simply piled up as they came out of production. 'It's extraordinary how badly furniture has been sold in this country,' said Conran. 'In those days the furniture stores were loaded with a huge variety of different styles. They did nothing convincingly.'

Like it or loathe it, Conran's style is nothing if not convincing, and when he opened the first Habitat in 1964 he met a demand that had been waiting to be satisfied.

'There was that strange moment round about the mid-60s when people stopped needing and need changed to want,' he said. 'Many things came together: the postwar generation were becoming consumers, there was a lot of media awareness of what was going on, and foreign holidays made people see how the other chap lived. Designers became more important in producing "want" products rather than "need" products, because you have to create the desire.'

That was the fertile ground Conran needed for his almost missionary belief that good design should be available for every consumer. As a manufacturer, which he continued to be for several years after Habitat started, he also realised how much influence a successful retailer could exert on suppliers by insisting on standards of quality and design.

He subsequently had to abandon manufacturing when he bought the Habitat shops out of an unhappy merger with Ryman in 1970, and he went over to the view that the two functions ought to be kept separate. He had discovered that other manufacturers were wary of supplying to Habitat. While it was and is a marvellous showcase, the fear was that he would always be tempted to give his own-made furniture first priority, which was a weakness in driving the hardest bargain with outsiders.

Conran claims that what he sees as an appalling cynicism still lurks in the darker corners of high streets. 'Retailing in this country has been blinded by store buyers saying the public will never be interested in this or that,' he said. 'The "They have no taste, they don't matter" type of thinking hasn't entirely gone away,' he said, 'but what you mustn't do is talk down to people, and now it is recognised that design is a part of retail power, part of the image you are trying to promote. We have put stores in places like Romford and found a large aspirational working class. Whoever said "retail is detail" was absolutely right. Next went through every detail – promotion, ticketing, labelling, uniforms – when I was launching it. The moment something jars the effect is lost.'

In recent years many retailers have tried themed tests in a corner of their stores, mirrored in the US by attempts at Lifestyle Departments. 'But they have been done with a total lack of conviction,' Sir Terence claimed. 'Half measures don't work, and that is true in life in general. You have got to do things with a total conviction. There is a tendency to see design as something of the moment. I obviously think it is much more fundamental than that. Everything that is made is designed, so why not make it good design backed by market research and with a degree of aesthetics? As creative retailers, our policy simply amounts to a belief that if reasonable and intelligent people are offered products for their home that are well made, well designed, work well, are of a decent quality and at a price they can afford, then they will like and buy them.'

That is how Habitat has been run from day one. It sounds simple, even amateurish. But Conran is far from that. He has a clear method for turning a new retail idea into reality, or getting the most out of an acquired business. He believes in starting with market research, to find out what the customer wants or is unhappy about. That leads to a design policy and a product range that fits that policy. The people are then recruited to put those decisions into practice – a process that can in itself take about a year. The shops are built or refurbished and the retail, personnel and stock control systems installed. Then the publicity machine wheels into action to tell the public all about it.

'The retailing systems are the most important part of the business,' he said, 'perhaps even more important than the design. The point of sale, the stock control, the delivery system, these are what matter. At Habitat we are usually five per cent out of stock, whereas most retailers are about fifteen per cent out.' That degree of control has been sharpened since the merger with BhS. A group-wide information system extends from the head office above Heal's in Tottenham Court Road to every one of the more than 500 branches in the UK, as well as the distribution centres.

Those systems enabled Sir Terence to take an early decision to pull BhS out of food retailing. In December 1985 Storehouse's shareholders were told that 'BhS's food ranges are being developed, particularly in the areas of natural foods, frozen foods and wine.' But by June 1986 the message in the annual report was: 'When BhS embarked on a new food strategy in 1984, it set a three-year trading profit objective. It has become clear that this target will not be met and therefore we have decided to withdraw from food retailing.'

Nevertheless, however carefully Conran tries to prepare his ground, even he can misjudge his market. In 1986 he also ran down Mothercare's Now chain of teenage fashion shops, after less than three years' trading. Arguably the irreversible decline of Now would not have been spotted so quickly without the ability to monitor the flow of stock on a day-to-day basis. But it also showed that even Conran's remarkable flair can occasionally let him down.

Now has been lit upon by some critics not only as Conran's first failure, but also as a possible shadow over the past twenty years' wisdom of targeting retailing operations at a predetermined audience. Rather than concede the broader doubts, Conran prefers to admit specific mistakes in the handling of Now. It began as an extension of Mothercare, where the age range stops at ten. The first outlets were adjoining Mothercare sites and took the age range up from ten to sixteen, a fickle group at the best of times. But with parents calling the tune the cash registers ticked over satisfyingly.

The trouble began when the Now chain branched out away from Mothercare's protective wing into stand-alone high street fashion locations. The 10-16s were no longer being pulled in by their parents, and older shoppers could not find clothes to fit them. Belatedly, the sizes were increased, but by then it was too late. 'Kids appeared to want to turn their backs on Mothercare when buying clothes,' said Conran. 'We had to decide whether to go on with an operation where we knew we had made mistakes or whether to learn from our errors and start again from scratch.' He has decided to start again with a clean sheet, aiming this time at the ficklest group of all, young fashions.

While that is a major challenge for the Conran design team, their greatest long-run task is to lift BhS in the public's mind to something more than a poor relation of Marks & Spencer. The process was already under way before the Habitat-BhS merger happened in 1985. The former management had been trying out new layouts since 1982, and before the merger Conran's people were acting as design consultants. A facelift has duly been applied, and the layout altered in an effort to get more people to perform the sometimes remarkably difficult trick of walking through the stores and opening their wallets at the same time.

One weekend in September 1986 the Conranisation of BhS began in earnest. A new logo was unveiled, incorporating what Sir Terence referred to as a flying 'h' between a more solid capital 'B' and 'S'. Some 6,000 triangular pillars, each about eight feet high, were installed in the 124 stores. Conran called them Exclamations. They signposted the different departments, and were used to illustrate the merchandise. Another 125,000 mood boards were pinned on the walls to add to the effect. Mood boards carry imaginative photographs of the goods and try to encourage the buying impulse. The result was to make the stores look livelier, less predictable, more attractive to the 25-year-olds as well as their mothers. The exercise gave Conran the excuse to run an advertising campaign which in effect said 'BhS has changed. Come and try it.'

Conran admitted: 'You have to change the culture right the way through the store. It is incredibly difficult to get rid of the "Are You Being Served" mentality. You have to have areas of excitement around your floorspace. BhS and M & S have walkways signposted to the different departments. We are going back to the micro situation of more personal retailing rather than the macro vision of the 1950s, of bowling people over with sheer size.'

Like his closest rivals, Sir Ralph Halpern at Burton Group and George Davies at Next, Conran is beginning to face his greatest challenge: whether the design-led strategy can be extended beyond what are essentially chains of boutiques into the heartland of the big-city high streets: the department stores. Mothercare and BhS are very similar. They both had good systems and a good structure to build on. Davies wanted to leap into that league by buying the House of Fraser chain, minus Harrods, but was denied. Halpern already has Debenhams. All three are trying to see if smart design and accurate targeting can turn department stores into the retail success story of the 1980s. Their success or otherwise in reaching that goal will have a profound influence on the shape of the high street between now and the end of the century.

'AND FOR MY NEXT TRICK'

Next is a butterfly of a company which has emerged from the caterpillar that was J. Hepworth, a Leeds-based business which, like Burton, made and retailed men's suits. But men do not wear suits so often these days, so both groups had to adapt or die. Burton's answer, under Sir Ralph Halpern, has been to build on its menswear base to develop a wide-ranging series of clothing shops for both men and women, as well as moving into department stores with the takeover of Debenhams. In a sense Hepworth is following a similar direction, but in more drastic fashion. Renamed Next, it has shed its old identity and simply does not exist in its former guise. But it sells men's and women's clothes, along with much else, and nearly bought the House of Fraser department stores early in 1986 – Harrods excepted.

The catalysts for the conversion of Hepworth into Next were Sir Terence Conran and George Davies, an exuberant Liverpudlian who cut his retailing teeth at Littlewoods and does not quite seem to believe his luck at being in the right place with the right idea at the right time. There appears to be little love lost between the two men, possibly because their contributions to the early development of Next were so closely intertwined. The original concept belongs to Davies, but Conran's designs put flesh on the shop concept and it was John Stephenson, a close associate of Conran, who is credited with dreaming up the name – a stroke of genius in itself, as many imitators have confirmed by their very act of imitation. He had thought of 'Next' as long ago as 1977, but had not found the right retail vehicle for it.

Davies recalled: 'Hepworth wanted to diversify away from menswear and had in mind to buy a small chain of women's clothes shops called Kendalls. They asked me to write a report on a concept that some of us had been kicking around at Pippa Dee, just over a pint, that sort of thing. It was an idea for a chain of shops selling what I call affordable collectables, retailing a whole range of complementary products that co-ordinate with one another and give the customer the ability to build a quality fashion statement over a season. I wrote this paper in 1981 and brought my team of people with me from Pippa Dee. The Next concept has not changed since then, though it has been considerably refined.'

Sir Terence Conran was then a non-executive director of Hepworth, and later became chairman, so it was natural that Conran Associates, as it then was, should do the design work for Next. 'I knew the products' design, but not the shop design,' said Davies. 'I believe that design has to be led by the retailer. The design expresses the concept.' But at that stage the new project lacked a name that would be sufficiently different to sum up its freshness and originality. Davies recalled how John Stephenson tried out the 'Next' name on him.

He said: 'Stephenson phoned me up and said "I think I've got the name you're looking for. Have you got a pencil and paper?" I said, "OK, I'm waiting." Then he spelt out N, E, X, T. I said "Is that it? Next?" But of course he was right. It meant things happening, and not just then but tomorrow. And it was so odd it made people remember it. I got home and asked my daughter, who was about seventeen then. She said "It's a terrible name, no good at all." That made me a bit miffed, but I asked her again a few hours later. She still said it sounded terrible, but the point was it had stuck in her mind, and that was what impressed me. Next has set a trend ever since, Before Next, most people called their shops by the name of the owner. We were the first to call it by an idea.'

Until Next cropped up, Conran had had no direct involvement in the fashion industry, but soon afterwards he resigned from Hepworth and went on to launch Now and buy Richards, which put him in competition with Davies. The fight was on for the hearts and minds of the modern lifestyle consumer, using design as the principal weapon.

'The funny thing was that Hepworth said that if they bought Kendalls I could run it, but if they didn't get it they would just pay me a fee for writing the report. I couldn't understand that. If I find someone who seems to know what he or she is talking about, I want to hang on to them, because you can always find a slot for them somewhere. Anyway, they did take over Kendalls. And it wasn't just a question of doing a refit. It was the biggest change ever – we converted seventy stores to Next in six weeks. We built all the shopfitting equipment off-site and put it in overnight. Getting things off the ground is hard work, and you need a lot of luck. But they let me get on with it. If they hadn't, I'd have left.'

What Davies discovered, and no one has so far been able to replicate to quite the same extent, is that Next is an infinitely flexible name. It can be applied to any retail theme, whether it is flowers, fabrics, furniture, cosmetics, crockery, cutlery, cafés, hairdressing, shoes, accessories, kids' clothes or anything else that sells and is consistent with the overall image of the group. Some companies have a far wider range, but are often more passive as retailers, taking something that a manufacturer has produced and giving it some space in the shop to sell it in. 'We look at products,' Davies insisted. 'We would take a table, if we wanted to sell tables, and put it in our style before it went on display.'

Like French Connection and one or two other groups, Next draws heavily on the output of design colleges, putting students to work in the company's design rooms and those of its suppliers to make sure the message gets across. And the quality back-up is there, too. Next claims to sample nearly 3,000 different cloths and yarns each season, each of which is tested under laboratory conditions for six months. From the sample fewer than fifty will be selected.

Davies first extended the Next theme, reasonably enough, from women's to men's fashions. 'I like challenges,' he said, 'that's what I need, that constant thing, almost to prove we can take it further. The initial 25 per cent compound growth broadened my horizons and the next thing was Next for Men. I saw how much Hepworth were taking, doing badly. Now if someone is doing something badly and you think you can do it better, then you do it. Next for Men got us on the road to the other products.'

The women's wear chain, 230 strong, has already been spun off into Next Collection for classic clothes and a more casual Next Too. Lingerie is another target. Similar fragmentation is likely for the men's side, and Davies has his eye on the shoe trade. 'We enjoy looking at areas like shoes,' he said, 'because I think that's been very badly managed as a sector up till now. We are beginning to sell them through Next Accessories, which also has handbags, belts and shirts.'

Quite apart from the group's own original ideas of which there have been plenty, such a chameleon-like strategy makes it relatively easy for Next to steal others' clothes. In 1986 it launched a cosmetic and skin care range concentrating heavily 'on purity and quality rather than just packaging, and many of the formulations will be vitamin-enriched.' Echoes of The Body Shop, maybe?

The logical high-street conclusion of splitting and multiplying the basic concept is a Next department store, and some of the different variations on the theme have indeed been grouped together under one roof. The point is that in a stand-alone shop you have got to be selling fast-moving goods to cover the overheads, and that sets strict limits on the range you can stock. It costs Next £350,000 a year to rent just 1,800 sq ft on the corner of Bond Street and Oxford Street in London. But the equation changes with department stores. 'Back space costs less than the space at the front,' Davies explained, 'so by combining the two you can give breadth of offer, which makes the whole company strong and the average rent lower.'

However, in 1986 Davies stepped beyond the property straitjacket by taking over Grattan, the mail-order house. 'Mail order' is no more as far as Next is concerned. Now it is 'home shopping'. That gives Davies the opportunity to spread the Next gospel without paying high-street rents, using the mailing lists of Grattan and Club 24, Next's credit operation, to reach the public through smartly redesigned catalogues and video tapes. Nearly half of British households have a video recorder, and they are by and large the half that Davies wants to sell to.

David Jones, Grattan's chief executive, said: 'Mail order used to be about giving credit, but it changed when credit was no longer mail order's monopoly. Virtually all the big store chains have their own credit cards. And after Next and others, our catalogues looked very dowdy. We had to improve our merchandise offer.

What I feel excited about with Next Home Shopping is that we can increase the catchment area of mail order. We want to get a new customer base, using the Next name and new technology.'

Those two tools can be cross-fertilized to powerful effect. The catalogues, or their Davies-inspired successors, can be targeted even more precisely than the shops, using the Grattan database, which tells head office who is buying what size and style of each item. Fat, thin, tall, short, rich, poor, young and old men and women, from Yuppies to Fogies, will be accurately identified and sold to. The appropriate catalogues can be stocked in their matching branches of Next, just like Mothercare and Habitat do, and the shops can be promoted through the home shopping material.

'Retailing is about believing in an idea, it's about young people with energy and a belief,' said Davies. 'In retailing you have to have a vision and when I started Next my aim was to make a bit of money for the group and do something I would enjoy doing. Marks & Spencer have had a fantastic influence on me. You couldn't help admire their single-mindedness in developing their style, and that was an important point that I have kept in mind in developing Next. We are more entrepreneurial than M & S, but they are a bigger and older company. The great thing is that there's room always for the new person. Retailing doesn't always go by size. It's not about figures and balance sheets, though they're important to show the results of your efforts. It's a business where people stamp their personalities, in the ideas they have and how they go about them.'

On Next's record, that theory suggests Davies is innovative and restless, someone who does not want to be pigeonholed. The shift into Next Too and Next Collection sprang out of a fear that Burton, Richards and Marks & Spencer were closing in on the original Next chain, and that Next was beginning to look too much like them. Rather than be caught with a huge bill for redesigning the shops, he cleverly chose to change the stock instead, so that women's expectations were altered accordingly.

The question is how often Davies can repeat that diversionary tactic. Me-too is the oldest trick in the retailing book, and one that Davies has a near-obsession about being hit by. 'I've been aped by every major retailer,' he said, 'so if anyone thinks I'm going to reveal my inner thoughts, they'd be wrong.' But however secret he keeps his plans, the day has to come when each of them is launched into the marketplace and subjected to the scrutiny of the competition as well as the consumer. If they work, the copycats soon come running.

But perhaps Davies' secret is that he often does not know what he himself is going to come up with. He is far more liable to change his mind than, say, Sir Terence Conran. In the summer of 1986, when he was taking over Grattan for £800 million, his face was set against concessions, the system whereby a retailer lets out space in his shops to another retailer, usually with a specialisation. The two approaches can complement one another and the shopowner collects rent. 'But,' said Davies in July 1986, 'We must check out ourselves the design/quality/price equation. We cannot leave anything to others. Marks & Spencer have that integrity. That is my model.' Less than four months later he was admitting that he had been 'rethinking' concessions: 'Done well, they could add something to the store,' he mused. And if he does not know what he is going to be doing, how can his competitors second-guess him?

Just as Next relies on impulse purchases, so it is driven by apparently impulsive decisions from the top. But that is all right. It helps to preserve the spontaneity which keeps the shoppers coming back just to see what the group is up to, and helps to ward off the bureaucracy that Davies is so afraid of. The beauty of the formula is that it is supple enough to be whatever he wants it to be, and design is just part of the armoury he uses to woo his customers.

Fast Footwork in Store

THE PROTAGONISTS:
- *HOUSE OF FRASER*
- *DEBENHAMS*

Department stores have been the high street's white elephants, unloved but impossible to ignore. One of the biggest questions in British retailing is whether they can become gazelles again. They have from the beginning been an outlandish hybrid of commerce and show business. Their original rationale was rooted in the huckster's desire to bang the drum and bring the crowds running. Although church architecture demonstrated that department stores were technically possible centuries before their time, they needed the support of a rising middle class who could pay the prices a department store needs to charge to pay for its structural largesse.

Logically, they should have prospered as living standards rose and the middle class, however defined, became the biggest part of the population. But they failed to keep up with the times, allowing specialist chains to take up the running. The department stores' biggest asset, their sense of occasion, of something more than a mere shopping trip, was with a few notable exceptions dissipated as managements neglected to spend the money necessary to maintain the sense of showbiz. Instead many became rather dusty relics of their former glory, culminating in the closure of their progenitor, Whiteleys of Bayswater, west London. A visit to Whiteleys had become a drab and depressing experience rather than the event it was designed to be.

Department stores had been left behind by social change. By the 1960s there were better things to do for entertainment than take a bus or train up to town and traipse round the counters of a run-down memorial to times past. More shoppers preferred to use their car. Most department stores had been built before the age of mass motoring and so did not carry facilities for large-scale parking. Even Harrods, the Rolls-Royce of the trade, came to depend on tourists because there was no longer enough local custom to pay for its long, long Knightsbridge frontage and top-hat prices.

One problem was that innovation in retailing had come upwards from the bottom. It is a business that does not need a great deal of starting capital at a simple level, and once the key department store sites had been claimed by the early years of this century there was neither the scope nor the inclination to produce new competitors. Any retailer with ambitions towards large scale began to look to out-of-town sites, which provided a different type of shopping experience from the old department stores and offered easy parking into the bargain. The American shopping mall became another model for the new breed of retailers and property developers, where the same effect as a high street could be conjured under an all-in roof. Department stores had little answer except to join the new trend.

The department stores are the enigma of the modern high street. They began as the great innovation in retailing, using sheer size to tell the public that they had the answer to every shopper's every whim. A company that could erect one of these giant emporia, like Harrods or Selfridges or Marshall & Snelgrove, oozed the promise that it was reliable, dependable, offering high quality goods with a grandeur that had not been seen before. They effectively invited shoppers to immerse themselves in the atmosphere of luxury and opulence they skilfully created. But they were appealing to a particular sector of the public. They were aimed at the middle classes, who had the time and money to stroll round the stores, but might not be able to afford the really expensive bespoke shops. As such they were an exercise in illusion for most of their customers.

A wealthy few do indeed still go to these stores to furnish their homes from top to bottom, usually putting the bills on their account as they go. But most buy one or two items and think how nice it *would* be to be able to have everything else they see. A large proportion in effect go sightseeing, not troubling the cash till at all.

When the American-born Gordon Selfridge opened his Oxford Street store in 1909 his publicity described shopping there as 'A Pleasure – A Pastime – A Recreation' and added: 'We aim to make the shopping at Selfridges something more than merely shopping. We would like to think that everyone who spends an hour or a day beneath our roof is better for the experience, has seen many "things different", has gathered some new point of knowledge, has discovered a way to do something better and revealed the thought to us. This is part of our ambition, and what we know will come about by cordial "entente" between Customers and ourselves.' The 'cordial entente' phrase was a reference to the Entente Cordiale, which had recently been signed by Britain and France. But such a soft-sell approach, as it would now be regarded, required the assumption that enough of those spending an hour or a day under Mr Selfridge's roof would be sufficiently beguiled to spend a little money as well. They obviously did, and do, for the store is still going strong.

The major change for department stores in the past forty years has been the nature of the competition it faces. Not from other department stores, because they tend to keep a respectful distance from one another, but from the rash of new high-street ventures to tempt shoppers. While much of the newcomers' appeal has been to the mass market, inevitably they have syphoned off some of the business which would have been taken by the department stores. They have been more in tune with the times, and visits to out-of-town warehouses have to some extent replaced the department stores' role as a provider of a day trip. So the big stores have had to play to their strengths by offering a wide range of high quality furnishings, clothes and accessories under one roof. These are the sorts of goods that carry a higher profit margin and may not face as much competition a few doors down the street.

But their biggest asset is the shopping experience they can give. That means spending plenty of money regularly and frequently to keep the store looking special, rotating displays and promotions to retain a sense of surprise, so that shoppers will want to keep coming back to see what's happening next. They have to play on human curiosity. Once they lose that, like poor old Whiteleys in its later years, the public stays away. They decide they can get what they want elsewhere, and the reason for making that special visit gradually disappears.

Department stores have something in common with grand restaurants, in that they have to offer a complete shopping menu to back their claim to be comprehensive. Most restaurant meals come down to prawn cocktail, steak and a gâteau, but diners like to feel that they could choose something more exotic if they wanted to. In the same way, the perfume, clothes and furnishing departments account for most of a store's trade and others, such as pets or books, will not clock up anything like the sales per square foot that fashion does, but the management must think long and hard before they close any of these extra attractions.

Groceries or a cafeteria are two food areas which have come under increasing pressure. Many people now buy groceries in a one-stop visit to the nearest supermarket, and they can always get a cup of coffee at McDonald's. That challenges the contribution these activities used to make in building traffic, drawing shoppers into the department store. While one or two exceptions like Harrods' Food Halls have maintained their status several grades above a mere supermarket, elsewhere stores have given up the fight and looked for something else to pull in the customers.

But the recent power struggle between the Al-Fayed brothers and Lonrho's Tiny Rowland over House of Fraser, the Harrods company, showed that department stores can still exert an overwhelming fascination for the businessman. It lies in the intangible asset that a really successful department store can create: its name, reputation, even aura. These are weapons that entrepreneurs spend years trying to compile, and there is almost no price they will not pay to acquire them off the peg as long as they belong in a business the would-be owner feels he can master.

The alternative is to pick up a big name that has fallen on hard times and make a fortune by restoring it to its former glory. That, in essence, is what Sir Ralph Halpern is attempting to do with Debenhams, a company that was clinging to its independence in the face of periodic takeover bids until Sir Ralph's Burton Group mounted a successful siege in 1985. While the new management at House of Fraser is largely concentrating on the orthodox solutions to that company's problems, Sir Ralph is determined to bring Debenhams back to centre stage with a succession of firework displays. Between these two, and the responses they must provoke from their rivals, department stores are likely to be more exciting places to visit in the 1990s. But it remains to be seen whether they can recapture the proud share of retailing turnover that they held in their heyday.

HARRODS AND THE HOUSE OF FRASER

For the past generation House of Fraser's fate as a company has been tied to the coat-tails of Harrods, arguably the world's most famous department store. As Harrods was fought over in its days as an independent concern, so Fraser became a corporate battleground largely because it won the fight for Harrods. The machinations are worth recalling because they show what men will do to secure the glittering power of a name like Harrods. They also suggest that department stores may not be the bygone relic of the high street that they were once believed to be.

In the 1950s Lord Fraser, the founder and chairman of House of Fraser, wanted to buy Harrods to make it the jewel in his crown, the confirmation of his place in posterity as the department store king of his day. And the prize was there for the taking. By that time it was run by Sir Richard Burbidge, grandson of Charles Harrod's general manager, a pleasant man but without any taste for the stock market takeover contests that had been sparked off after the war by Sir Charles Clore. Harrods had acquired Dickins and Jones and D H Evans in London, Kendal Milne in Manchester, John Walsh in Sheffield, J F Rockhey in Torquay, and other provincial department stores in the early years of this century.

But by 1959 it was itself ripe for being taken over and it became the subject of a stock market auction by Fraser and Debenhams. Sir Richard naively pleaded with the Harrods staff to buy shares in the company to stave off the marauders, but Lord Fraser knew that this might be his only chance to acquire the Knightsbridge store and its outposts. His determination was decisive. When he won he said: 'This is all I have ever wanted.'

Lord Fraser died in 1966 and was succeeded by his son, Sir Hugh, an amiable heir then only 29 who became staple fodder for the gossip columns and also had a weakness for gambling. In the mid-1970s he began to fall under the influence of the mercurial Roland 'Tiny' Rowland, chief executive of Lonrho, the international trading group. Both had by then been the subject of official censure, Rowland being famously described by Edward Heath as 'an unacceptable face of capitalism', and Sir Hugh for his stock market dealings. However unacceptable Heath may have found him, Rowland is a man who can wield immense personal charm. He once said: 'I have an instinct, a deep animal instinct, for the chemistry of people.' He befriended Sir Hugh, who grew to regard him almost as a father figure.

It only gradually became clear to the outside world that a prime motive behind Rowland's friendliness was what turned out to be an almost obsessive desire to own Harrods. He bought a large block of shares in Scottish and Universal Investments, using that in 1979 as a springboard to buy the whole company. Among other things, it in turn owned thirty per cent of the shares in House of Fraser. Rowland was so excited by this coup that the following year the Lonrho annual report contained no fewer than five colour pictures of Fraser stores – including, of course, Harrods.

Rowland duly became a director of House of Fraser, but the relationship between him and Sir Hugh blew hot and cold. Sir Hugh realised that he was in danger of losing control of the group his father had bequeathed to him, and there were doubts as to whether he had sufficient steel in his bones to see off the challenge. He did not, and the torch was passed to Roland Smith, Professor of Marketing at Manchester University and an experienced company 'doctor'. Smith is one of the most stubborn men to sit at the table of any boardroom in Britain.

Smith kept Rowland at bay, despite not one but two full-scale takeover bids by Lonrho. Each was held up by Monopolies and Mergers Commission investigations, the first of which thwarted the proposed deal. In between the two bids, Rowland tried a succession of manoeuvres to get his hands on Harrods. One was to argue that as it was so distinct from the rest of House of Fraser, it should be floated off on the stock market as a separate company. Once floated, it could then have been open to a frontal attack by Rowland.

But by an extraordinary twist Rowland was denied his prize at the death. The second bid, in 1984, prompted a second official inquiry. When the Monopolies and Mergers Commission was given leave by the Government to extend its scrutiny for a further three months, Rowland's patience snapped. He sold Lonrho's thirty per cent stake in Fraser to Mohamed, Ali and Salim Al-Fayed, three brothers of Egyptian origin who were in shipping and import-export, and owned the Ritz Hotel in Paris. They were former associates of Rowland: in 1975 they had held £7 million of shares in Lonrho, and Mohamed Al-Fayed had briefly been a director.

Evidence is scanty on precisely why Rowland sold. But the Egyptians went on to make a bid of their own for the whole of Fraser – which succeeded, untrammelled by official investigations. Rowland was furious, but powerless. His instinct for the chemistry of people had for once let him down.

The Al-Fayeds have talked about franchising the Harrods

name, setting up a branch in every leading city in the world. 'There is no reason why, if it is properly handled, it should not be like the Holiday Inn hotels chain,' said Ali. 'We would lay down the rules for running a Harrods store anywhere in the world.' But their first priorities were to make sure that the Knightsbridge original was performing smoothly, and then to bring the other 101 stores in the Fraser group up to scratch.

In 1986 Professor Smith stepped down, to make way for a young Australian called Brian Walsh, who had been managing director of David Jones, a company running forty department stores in Australia and fifteen in the US. He became chief executive of the Egyptian-controlled House of Fraser. 'I guess they picked me because I was the best man for the job,' he said jauntily. He brings a fresh eye to the business of running department stores, and may have been regarded as the best man for the job because he has a healthy scepticism about the standard of retailing in Britain. 'I don't see what's happening here as a retail revolution,' he explained, 'but more of an evolution. This country had not moved to catch up with what had been going on in the rest of the world. Too many of the shops here have been of a very poor standard and very poor quality. It's the retailing of the 1940s.'

A broom like that is clearly going to sweep more than a few cobwebs away in a group as sprawling as House of Fraser. 'It would be pretty dumb to make them all Harrods,' Walsh pointed out, 'because there just isn't the market for it elsewhere in the country. There wouldn't be enough people using it. You have to tailor your business to the market.'

There is a managing director for each House of Fraser division, north, south and midlands, with separate divisions for Harrods, Dickins and Jones and the Copenhagen store Illum. They have discretion within the guidelines Walsh sets them. He is autocratic. They run promotions and hire and fire staff, and they have to meet financial targets, but Walsh tells them how he wants the stores run.

About eighty per cent of what Fraser stocks is the same throughout the country. The other twenty per cent is changed to take account of different standards of living and regional variations. 'You've got a considerable climatic difference from one end of the country to the other, and the store has to be identified with the local people,' said Walsh. 'You've got such a rich variety of accents and cultures within this island, and it would be a pity to lose that, to have a bland sameness everywhere. Some of the sites we operate are too small to offer a full range of department store facilities. We are looking at turning them into speciality shops. Some are badly in need of renovating. About half are first-rate. Illum in Copenhagen has a huge dome and the central area is completely open up to the roof, with escalators, just like the new galleria that Halpern is building at Debenhams. Fraser's in Glasgow is one of the most beautiful stores I've seen, again with a big dome. It's been run down, but I'm going to bring it back up. There's nobody else that has the capacity we have.'

As far as Walsh is concerned, Britain is all about high streets, making it totally different from his experience in the US and Australia, where retailing is all about the subtle technique of encouraging people to spend in shopping malls. 'I used to think that was a disadvantage about Britain,' Walsh admitted, 'but the great thing is that all the other shops in the high street look the same. You can make a department store very distinctive. They are a part of show business.' And that means persuading people to buy things they don't need, whether it's a new shirt, a new dress or a new set of curtains.

'The general principles of department stores are the same everywhere,' Walsh explained. 'I've travelled a lot, and it's the same wherever you go. You put the perfume counter in the front of the ground floor. That's where you always find the Estée Lauder. Then handbags and jewellery. Household goods you put up on the third floor, because they tend to be a family purchase – the husband and wife come in on a Saturday. We do the usual things to get people up on to the higher floors. We put the ladies' toilet on the top floor, and other services, to draw them up and let them filter down.'

The point is that 85 per cent of department store customers are women – but the stores are run by men. The result is that too many stores forget to think of things like whether the ladies' toilets are pleasant and clean. The same goes for the restaurant. A man may simply want a place where he can have a cheese sandwich and a cup of coffee: women will want a place that is comfortable enough for them to sit down and have some tea and a chat with their friends. And Walsh pointed out that often you find racks that are six feet high, because they've been installed by men. But women are only 5ft 4in tall on average, so they can't see over them. These are the things he is committed to putting right. 'Retail is detail is an old saying, but it's absolutely true,' he remarked. 'There are three golden rules: know your customer, give her what she wants, and give good service. There are plenty more of course, normal business rules, like knowing when to mark down merchandise that isn't selling, but you must have those three rules.'

What has most frustrated Walsh are the English salesperson's unwillingness to sell, and the amount of sales lost through being out of stock. When he first arrived to have a serious look at the Fraser outlets, he was rubbing his hands in anticipation because of the numbers of people walking through the stores. In that sense, Britain has a much higher density of traffic than elsewhere. But it is much harder to set that traffic ringing the tills.

'The shops here are spoilt for traffic, and it's only a question of converting a few more into sales,' said Walsh. 'But people are not as ready to sell here. I suppose it's the native reticence, but they find it hard to recognise the customer. Just say hello, that's all you have to do. You must make contact. It doesn't really matter what you say, what a nice child you've got, whatever. Once you've made that contact you've got them. You're much more likely to make a sale. It's not a question of ignoring them versus badgering them, it's shades of grey. People say to me here, "We don't like to hassle the customer". That's all right: you don't have to hassle them. Just be nice to them. Service is just being nice to people. You think of a time when you had really good service: all it came down to was that the person was nice to you. If you have that you can get away with anything. If you haven't got it, you'd better find something else to do.' Of course financial incentives can do much to shape a salesperson's outlook, and Walsh has been looking at ways of restructuring the House of Fraser commission system.

The other war Walsh is waging is on the amount of business the group loses through being out of stock, usually on the best-selling line in a department. This largely stems from the way store buyers have traditionally ordered goods. They often ask for so many in each size and colour, no matter which is selling well, then inevitably the most popular goes first.

'It's hard to get them to think in terms of stocking up the best lines,' said Walsh. 'People don't realise how many sales are lost through being out of stock. Take thread: white and black thread outsell any other colours by a huge margin. But you go to the thread counter and I promise you'll see the whole range of colours, golds and yellows and reds – and one reel of white and one of black!'

Harrods, Walsh readily admits, is in a different class from the rest of Fraser's stores – even if it does not order enough reels of black thread. Because of its unique name, jealously guarded by prosecutions against anyone who attempts to steal it, great care must be taken in making any changes. And it is no longer just a piece of retailing show business, like any other department store. Harrods ranks with Buckingham Palace and the Tower of London as a must on any tourist's itinerary, to the extent that half its £300 million-a-year turnover comes from overseas visitors. They are looking for the things that make Harrods special, not for its inevitable similarities with lesser establishments.

Two problems constantly assail Harrods' management. Despite the British unemployment level, it is increasingly difficult to maintain the standard of service that prevailed in times gone by. Customers expect perfection, and complain sooner than they would elsewhere if they get the merely adequate. Secondly, the store occupies the whole of the island site and the building is over 100 years old, so does not lend itself easily to modification.

'I wish the escalators at Harrods were in the middle, but they are at either end,' Walsh moaned. As well he might: the second set of escalators was installed only in 1981, though they are supplemented by lifts at the heart of the building. 'We are working on ways to see how we can open it up so that you can see all round,' he explained. 'At the moment it is a lot of small rooms. We have a major traffic problem within the store. There is a lot of waste space, and we may open up more of the subterranean area.' Until 1983 the public was unaware of the existence of the huge warren that runs under Brompton Road to the supply depot at Trevor Square. Then the Food Halls were extended to the lower ground floor for cookery demonstrations, a coffee counter, health food and a small supermarket. That way the department store principle of 'everything under one roof' was maintained. It would not be quite the same to cross the street to shop in a Harrods annexe.

But unless the ownership of Harrods changes yet again, we are unlikely to see anything as daring as a share shop opening there, even though its ground-floor banking hall was famous for many years. In fact, Walsh is sceptical of the whole fashion for bringing financial and other services into department stores. 'I'm not a great believer in bringing in travel agencies, opticians, that sort of thing, into department stores,' he said. 'People go to a department store primarily to shop and they might see the services, but basically the services and concessions live off the store. Retailers do that at their peril. I believe in sticking to what you know. There's been too much encouragement of concessions.'

DEBENHAMS, GALLERIA STYLE

Debenhams, all 67 stores and 6.7 million sq ft, is at a crossroads. Or as its new leader, Sir Ralph Halpern, would put it, the stores have just left the crossroads and are embarking down a completely new path. The moment of decision, at least for Debenhams' then shareholders, was the takeover bid in 1985 by Sir Ralph's company, Burton Group. It was not the first time someone had attempted to take Debenhams over. UDS tried and failed in 1972.

Halpern fought on the platform that the department store chain needed to be taken in a completely new direction to bring it up to date with what has been happening in retailing. He won, but we have yet to see his vision bear fruit.

The most controversial aspect of Halpern's vision was his galleria concept, where the centre of a store would be gouged out to leave the departments ranged around the sides in a gallery formation. At its most lavish, like the San Francisco branch of Saks Fifth Avenue, escalators are installed in the central atrium so that shoppers' eyes are caught by displays as they travel up and down.

Some of Halpern's critics argued that it was too expensive to convert existing buildings to the galleria style – possibly £10 million per store. Others said, look at the selling space you have to give up to create the atrium, maybe as much as a third of the total: the remainder has to work half as hard again to make that up. Yet others dismissed the idea as old hat. Britain is littered with veteran department stores featuring a central well leading up to a chandeliered dome, even if customers were expected to walk a staircase to get the full effect. However, the idea was sufficiently startling – even if it is limited to the Oxford Street store – to convince normally sceptical fund managers holding Debenhams shares that Halpern could and would inject some much-needed fresh ideas into a company that had gone stale.

The Oxford Street branch has been receiving the galleria treatment, but it is too early to say whether it has had the desired effect on sales, let alone profits. Unless the impact is dramatic, few other Debenhams outlets are likely to be converted in this way. They may have to make do with a more modest facelift and rearrangement of departments into more attractive and logical combinations.

Galleria were also part of the grand alliance between Halpern and Sir Terence Conran, an alliance which featured heavily in the takeover campaign. Full-page advertisements showed the two great men side by side. Although the bid was being made solely by Burton, the front cover of the formal document sent to Debenhams shareoulders gave equal billing to Conran's Habitat Mothercare, as if it was a joint offer by the two allies.

Sir Ralph explained at the time: 'After his own proposals to Debenhams were rebuffed, we began discussions with Sir Terence to add his talents to our own. These discussions, I am happy to say, have resulted in arrangements for the Habitat Mothercare group to work with us both to design new retail formats and to trade in Debenhams. Indeed, the successful conclusion of our negotiations with Habitat Mothercare shortly before the offers were announced was a material factor in our assessment of the potential value to us of Debenhams and in our decision to go ahead.'

It was a three-pronged agreement. Conran was to be allowed to take up to twenty per cent of Debenhams' trading space, be responsible for some of the redesign of the stores and be granted an option on twenty per cent of Debenhams' shares. But this harmonious relationship came to grief a few months later when Conran merged with British Home Stores, since renamed BhS. In Halpern's eyes that made him a direct competitor and invalidated the agreement. Fitch & Co. Design Consultants won the main contract instead.

More than a year after the Debenhams takeover, a compromise was eventually worked out. Instead of the Debenhams chain, Sir Terence would be given the 400 Burton Menswear shops to redesign. The only Debenhams outlet he would work on as part of the agreement would be Harvey Nicholls, round the corner from Harrods in Knightsbridge, but he would be allowed to take space elsewhere in the chain. The plan for a Conran shareholding in Debenhams was quietly dropped.

So the Halpern experiment in revitalising department stores got off to a bumpy start. Within six months, after he had had a chance to have a good look at the books, he declared: 'It will be two to three years before we start producing the kind of figures we are used to in Burton.' The deal not only tripled the amount of selling space at his command, he also had to dismantle the new management structure which Debenhams had erected only two or three years previously.

The idea had been to make each department pay its way by setting them up as separate group-wide subsidiaries and charging them market rent, as if they were concessionaires. Indeed, plenty of real concessions were sold, ironically including one to Dorothy Perkins, part of Burton Group. That enabled Halpern to rub Debenhams' noses in their shortcomings by claiming that over a four-month period the Perkins concession had achieved sales growth of seventeen per cent, nearly three times the increase achieved by Debenhams itself.

But the real problem was that the ten Debenhams trading subsidiaries were always in danger of being at one another's throats. Each was responsible for buying, selling, staff and making its own profit. So they were all competing with one another without sufficient overall direction or co-ordination. The stores had begun to look a mess.

That was completely contrary to Halpern's way of thinking. He lays some claim to having started the trend towards focused retailing in the 1970s, though in the more straightforward area of multiple retailing, where you can develop several chains with their own theme without the complications involved in combining them under one roof to form a coherent whole. Burton started creating chains of stores that catered for a particular market, based on the way the target audience lived. It was a way of getting away from the former emphasis on price, where Burton had sold

Sir Terence Conran unveiling the new BhS logo.

The Next look at a branch in Chester.

A more theatrical approach to the bedding department at
House of Fraser.

Either one could turn Debenhams round. You are being offered both of them.

Sir Ralph Halpern (top left) and Sir Terence Conran making their joint assault on Debenhams. . . . and (below) Sir Ralph's galleria takes shape.

suits as cheaply as possible because most people did not in those days aspire to be individualistic. They wanted something that would fit in with everyone else. The only escape from that, Halpern argued, was to concentrate on style, accurately targeted. So Burton begat or developed Peter Robinson, Top Shop, Top Man, Dorothy Perkins, Evans, Principles, Principles For Men, Fenton, Studio. Something for everyone, but not in each shop.

'Consumers are becoming more demanding, sophisticated and aspirational,' said Halpern. 'That last word is important. Before, the communications industry was poor, television just developing and you had not got the lifestyle images you get now. It's these that have made us feel we want a better life. The factory fodder existence came to an end with mass communications. People wanted better holidays, better food, more fun. Habitat and some of the restaurant chains met the need and gained market share. That was at the expense of others, because it was a static market. It was a case of the people's aspirations finding an outlet within that static market.'

Halpern, now a millionaire, has that secret quality of many successful businessmen: he springs from the market he sells to. He started as a Selfridges trainee then joined Burton at £15 per week, more than 25 years ago. The question is whether he can transfer that common touch to the problems of department stores.

'Department stores were a way of taking you away from the corner shop – Harrods sold everything from elephants to pyjamas – but those days have gone,' he said. 'If you try and stock anything and everything you lose out to those who focus their marketing. Allders and Debenhams do not compete with Dixons. Dixons' whole life is devoted to their area of the market. So department stores have tried to specialise themselves too. Food halls in the US have delicatessen and speciality food. Marks & Spencer sells tandoori chicken – prepared, focused. They take the trouble and the time for you. Their concept is to take a low margin area and make it high margin by taking the trouble out of it. Department stores will compete. Debenhams will sell fashionable products for the home and personal adornment, with the emphasis on "fashionable".'

Sensibly, Halpern is taking Debenhams out of the highly competitive specialisations like food and electricals. He wants to be in areas where he knows he can be as good as the best, and organise his stalls accordingly. Unlike Walsh at House of Fraser, he is taking his department stores into financial services in conjunction with others, and specialist services to the the consumer. Before the takeover, Debenhams had already provided space for the stock-broking firm of Quilter Goodison to run a share shop on the top floor of the Oxford Street branch, an exercise which proved highly successful. The aim is to make the chain as proficient as Sears Roebuck in the US.

'It's all about sustained competitive advantage,' said Halpern. 'You have to bring in new edges all the time. It's about making services more available to the consumer through anyone, to any-one. All the edges are becoming more blurred in retailing. And there will a be a greater concentration of power: those retailers who have not found a new formula will eventually fade away because they have not found a new mission. It's all about giving each chain a mission to reach and sell to a particular audience.'

Halpern expects that the methods used to reach those audi-ences will change out of recognition in the coming years, through the use of satellite television and electronics to enhance mail order. Satellite will pave the way for international marketing, so that shoppers will be able to order goods from the US through their television and pay for them by American Express or Visa.

Meanwhile, Halpern believes, retailing's move out of town still has some way to go. He foresees the growth of motorway crosses, like small towns sited at the points where motorways cross. And that will mean the high street will have to fight back even harder. 'There are not many attractive shopping areas in towns,' he said. 'High streets were made for carriages, not huge lorries. Traffic should be diverted. The high street is a social centre. Car parking has to be worked out on the basis of the number of cars per square foot of shopping. But in secondary areas property developers will create areas like Covent Garden, constructed out of old cinemas or bingo halls. They will not want Etam or Top Shop, but speciality shops.'

In the course of doing his bit to change the face of British retailing, Halpern has come in for his share of criticism over the system he has instituted for his own salary. Last year he became the first retailer, and one of the first businessmen in Britain, to receive £1 million. 'But that is because I do not have the share-holdings that the Sainsburys and the others have,' he explained.

'The Sainsburys get £5 million a year from their dividends. So I have developed a system of profit-related incentive on the basis of earnings per share. It's a kind of dividend. If the shareholders do better, I do better. One of the things we have to do is to change attitudes. I have to show it's worthwhile taking over as chairman of this company because you get money out of it. It's not just loyalty that we pay for.'

His hope is that others will join him in the £1 million-a-year club, and of course his dearest wish is that the British could lose their envy of high salaries and instead adopt the American attitude of regarding high salaries as a goal to emulate rather than a butt to deride. 'The status of retailing is competitive, exciting, entrepreneurial, it pays a lot of money and it has a future,' Halpern exclaimed. 'The whole status of retailing has changed in the last twenty years. Before it was just an occupation people took because there was no alternative for the unsophisticated. Now it's really high profile. One can make great progress in terms of career, money, recognition.'

Sir Ralph Halpern has the career and the money. Full-blooded recognition awaits his transformation of Debenhams into a chain of stores that everyone wants to be seen in.

A Tale of Two Cultures

THE PROTAGONISTS:
- *MARKS & SPENCER*
- *JOHN LEWIS PARTNERSHIP*

Every successful business is driven by an idea, often the result of a blinding flash of inspiration by its founder. He or she sees a gap in the market, perhaps something that is not being done as well as it should be, and takes the plunge. Only time tells whether that belief is commercially justified. However, among those enterprises which survive is a class apart: the ones where the skeleton is fleshed with a desire to be more than a business, perhaps to make a contribution to the community. Few can start with this ambition. Survival must be the first aim. But once the company has developed a life of its own, wider horizons beckon. Many entrepreneurs spend their lives trying to become dominant in their field, so that they can leave an established business to posterity and possibly earn a knighthood or a peerage for themselves. A large number donate thousands of pounds to charity each year. But a few feel strongly enough about their personal principles to want to put them into practice in their businesses.

John Lewis and Marks & Spencer are not the only examples of such companies, but they are the most vivid of the current crop. That they are both in retailing is no coincidence. It is a highly personal, highly labour-intensive industry, where systems can be laid down but where everyone from van driver to sales assistant plays a vital part. The goods have to be got to the shop on time and in mint condition. They have to be displayed tidily and attractively, and sold in a way that makes the customer want to come back for more. That encourages a positive attitude towards good employee relations, for an unwilling member of the team can mar the whole effort and cost a fortune in lost business.

Lewis and Marks have taken this perception further than anyone else on the high street. They have done so for very different reasons, and from historically different directions. Michael Marks' original penny bazaar had a small room over it where the staff could eat their sandwiches and make hot drinks. And when he built his first head office, in Manchester at the turn of the century, he installed a kitchen for staff to cook food and an adjoining room to eat it. But M & S took the question of staff facilities more seriously in the 1930s, after Simon Marks and his brother-in-law, Israel Sieff, found salesgirls not eating enough because their wage had to be divided amongst an otherwise unemployed family. Every store was then given its own staff kitchen and rest room.

Like Simon Marks, John Spedan Lewis was not the founder of his family's business. But unlike Marks, he went in the teeth of his father's opposition in pursuing his dream of building a company which would effectively be owned by its employees. In that, Lewis was far more radical than the Marks's. While both can be described as paternalistic, M & S has always proceeded on the orthodox lines of a limited company. It went public in 1927, and the ruling family still has a large number of shares, though small in relation to the total. More recently, the company has introduced an employee share scheme.

John Spedan Lewis, on the other hand, was determined to share profits with his employees as long ago as 1908. Just as M & S was finding its feet on the stock market, he was setting up an employee trust to buy the shares in the business. Upon that basic idea has been overlaid an elaborate framework of democratic power-sharing. Nevertheless, it is a remarkable testimony to the resilience of the founding family that the chairman is still a Lewis – just as, although the present chairman of M & S is from outside the family circle, there is still a Sieff and a Sacher on the board of that company. Both are directly descended from Michael Marks.

And the two companies leave no doubt that their apparent altruism has a hard commercial logic behind it. John Spedan Lewis saw the connection between a happy workforce and a prosperous business, and so did Simon Marks.

M & S is more famous for extending its philosophy to its suppliers, certainly after the Second World War, when the group had enough buying power to be able to tell manufacturers how to run their own businesses. This was particularly important in the food side of the business, where the standard of hygiene in industrial cooking could sometimes be frankly disgusting. The present Lord Sieff recalls seeing the floor of an oven room covered with red ants. That supplier did not last long.

While other retailers have turned the industry's former relations with suppliers on their head, it took a special type of self-confidence to blaze the trail. Maybe *chutzpah* would be a more accurate description: in business, today's *chutzpah* is tomorrow's accepted practice.

That self-confidence is a common characteristic of Marks and Lewis. The leaders of both companies seem to derive an inner strength from the set of beliefs they live by. The intriguing point, and this is certainly something that has puzzled the directors of John Lewis from time to time, is that few other companies take a leaf out of their book. After all, both Lewis and Marks disarmingly and at times infuriatingly stress the simplicity of their outlook. It boils down to value for money.

It is easier to dismiss the Lewis approach as a model for others. Money and then satisfaction are strong motives for most successful businessmen, and that satisfaction can be fully achieved only if it is accompanied by the levers of power. John Spedan Lewis may not have been quite unique but he was certainly a rarity in handing over his shareholding to an employee trust. Although the company did buy other retailers after that, the gesture has probably restricted its growth. The democratic process by which Lewis is governed makes it difficult to implement new strategic decisions quickly. The driving force of a single determined leader is diluted by the need to consult and consent.

M & S seems to have a more copiable formula. The chain of command at M & S has been much snappier and growth and changes of direction have been easier to achieve. What is not so easy is the time and care Marks puts into its principles. It is far too tempting for lesser mortals to rush in and cut corners.

Both companies have from time to time been bogged down by corporate caution. When the articles of faith are written on tablets of stone it can be difficult to persuade the elders that a new interpretation is consistent with that faith. Marks has had the occasional blitz on bureaucracy, and both chains still have a utilitarian air about them, despite recent attempts to brighten the stores. Their common aim of giving value for money has at times been a gentle curse. It is always ultimately the customers' money that is spent on a refurbishment programme, but few apart from Marks and Lewis are so ready to see it that way.

The more flamboyant style of rival retailers has produced more personal expression in their stores. The greatest threat to Marks and Lewis has been the design revolution. Neither has wanted to be at the forefront of fashion, which is in any case a risky and volatile business. But so fast have events moved in the past few years that the two chains have been in danger of being left behind. Their millions of faithful followers have stayed loyal, of course. But any thriving retail operation needs the constant infusion of new blood, most of which has to come from young shoppers.

Marks and Lewis acquired a reputation which also touched BhS until Sir Terence Conran applied his paint brush to it, as the stores for the new generation's mothers.

That is a problem which is all about market positioning, a subtle business which some retailers spend too much time on, ending up nowhere. Marks and Lewis shift their position almost imperceptibly, but when they move they move decisively. Lewis is not as strict as Marks about selling only under its own label, but neither has allowed any credit card but its own to sully their tills. In-store cards are proving the biggest sales boost since self-service, but these two vet new cardholders more rigorously than anyone else, seeing the exercise rightly as an extension of their image. Bad debts on cards can dent that image all too quickly.

Marks and Lewis have been just as careful with the move out of town. Both have happily taken space in shopping centres, which are really the high street in another guise, but both stress their continuing commitment to the high street. Only now are they gingerly planning stand-alone sites, and even here Marks prefers to develop in tandem with another retailer.

It may be that these two retailers are destined to remain the high street's successful anachronisms. They live by their own rules, almost but not quite disdaining the rough-and-tumble of the market place. They watch and examine trends carefully before deciding to join in, a luxury they can afford because of the numbers of customers for whom a shopping trip is not complete without a visit to one or other of Marks or Lewis.

They gain most of all from comparison shopping. Many people will use one or both of them as the yardstick by which to judge what is on offer elsewhere. The design may be better in another shop, or it may be cheaper, but the fact is that the competition often has to beat the Marks or Lewis comparison before they can secure the sale. That is an enviable position to be in, and one which neither group will lightly surrender.

NEVER KNOWINGLY UNDERSOLD

Step into a John Lewis store, and you enter a shrine. They all feed on the evangelism of retailing's most strongly principled, generous, selfless and cantankerous individual, John Spedan Lewis. Like his father, he laid down commandments for those who followed, the most sacred being 'the supreme purpose of the John Lewis Partnership is simply the happiness of its members.'

Spedan's father, plain John Lewis from Shepton Mallet, started as a draper's apprentice. At twenty he was the youngest silk buyer in London, working for Peter Robinson in Oxford Circus. Eight years later, in 1864, he opened his own drapery shop along the road in Oxford Street, site of the present store.

John's 21st birthday present to each of his two sons, Oswald and Spedan, was a quarter-share in the business. By then the fledgling retail empire had begun to take shape. John had bought a controlling stake in Peter Jones, the Sloane Square store, when Mr Jones died in 1905.

Spedan was to inherit those two stores and use them to bring to life his vision of a promised land. The effort to fulfil that vision has immortalised his name. He is the Founder, with a capital F, of the famous Partnership, with a capital P, which creates all employees equal. That is the basis of the John Lewis organisation today. It has no connection with Lewis's stores, which are owned by Sears.

Company folklore dates the genesis of Spedan's ideal back to 1908. Then 23, he was handed a copy of the firm's accounts and saw to his grief that the Lewis family was sharing a profit of £16,000, precisely equal to the total wages of the 300 employees. To the scorn and disgust of his father and brother, he began devising ways of dividing the proceeds more evenly.

Spedan explained in a 1957 radio interview: 'It was soon clear to me that my father's success had been due to his trying constantly to give very good value to people who wished to exchange their money for his merchandise. But it also became clear to me that the business would have grown further, and that my father's life would have been much happier, if he had done the same for those who wished to exchange their work for his money.'

Spedan seized the chance to test his ideas in 1914, when his father gave him control of the lossmaking Peter Jones. Nevertheless, Spedan went ahead with setting up staff committees and profit-sharing, when there were profits to be shared. The consequences for investors were unavoidable and dire. As he told the annual meeting of Peter Jones shareholders: 'The days when a lot of shareholders could stay at home doing nothing and take a very large proportion of the earnings of a business are all over.' He wasn't one to mince words.

The staff had to wait until 1920 for their first slice of the cake, not in cash but in preference shares. They were a doubtful gift. For the next few years, Peter Jones could not afford to pay dividends on those shares. But the precedent had been established, and Spedan had shown, to his own satisfaction at least, that his principles could be put into practice.

In 1926 Oswald gave Spedan his 25 per cent stake in the John Lewis store, effectively putting Spedan in control of both. Their father died two years later, and in the following year Spedan sold the business of John Lewis and Peter Jones to a trust in return for a £1 million interest-free loan repayable over thirty years.

Spedan kept a controlling stake through shares he held in John Lewis Partnership Limited, but he collected no dividends or salary for himself. Twenty-one years later, he signed another trust settlement which transferred ownership to the employees and set up the present machinery for running the business.

All the employees are known as partners, which means that every year on top of wages they receive a bonus calculated as a percentage of that salary. In recent years it has been as high as twenty per cent. But there is more to it than that. Through an elaborate system of checks and balances every partner today has a say in the business.

Although John Lewis Partnership is a public limited company, it is ultimately controlled by John Lewis Partnership Trust Limited. The chairman, currently Peter Lewis, a nephew of Spedan, holds forty per cent of the shares. The other sixty per cent is held jointly by three trustees, who can use their controlling vote only to remove the chairman.

The trustees are elected by a Central Council of 180, a fifth of whom are appointed by the chairman, the rest being elected by a secret annual ballot of all 28,000 partners. That body can direct the trustees to remove the chairman if a two-thirds majority of them decides he is no longer fit to hold that office. The Central Council also nominates five directors to the board of John Lewis Partnership plc. The chairman nominates another five, along with his own deputy, giving him effective day-to-day control. But he must give the council a yearly account of his activities and answer their questions. It is a unique system among major British companies.

One other unusual feature of John Lewis is the partnership's weekly Gazette and branch Chronicles. Any employee can write to them about whatever they please, anonymously if they prefer. They must all be published unless the chairman, no less, certifies that publication of a particular letter would be harmful to the partnership. Furthermore, all letters raising a question must be accompanied by a reply from a director or senior executive. If they are contentious enough, they frequently spark off a snarling reply from another partner in the next issue.

The partnership's doctrinal obsession with fairness can sometimes give way to nitpicking rules. Like most retail groups, John Lewis allows its staff discount on their in-house purchases. But those living with parents, grown-up children, friends or anyone else who cannot be classed as a dependant, are expected to scale down their discount accordingly. Only the spiritual descendants of Spedan could expect such self-denial. It can hardly be a coincidence that this ultra-democratic organisation should have elected the Founder's nephew as its current chairman.

The true faith in the partnership has preserved John Lewis' culture in a time warp stuck somewhere in the 1950s, the era when Spedan was irascibly relinquishing his orb and sceptre. While the corporate fashion has been to close sports grounds and other facilities bestowed in a more paternalistic era, John Lewis boasts a holiday camp, three country clubs and a hotel on Brownsea Island in Poole harbour.

They are the result of the paternalistic view that the partners' profits must be spent on recreation as well as bonuses. They are also some of the fruits of what is widely acknowledged to be among the most ruthless and unyielding trading policies known to the British high street.

The Lewis family realised early on that successful shopkeeping, on whatever scale, does not hinge on being clever. Instead, they preached the virtues of honesty, value and a wide assortment of stock, and clear identification of the market. 'Here you have all you need to know for successful trading,' said Spedan. 'The rest is application.'

The almost religious fervour with which those principles have been embraced, together with freedom from a posse of demanding shareholders, have allowed the group to sidestep the instant solutions to which retailing can so easily fall prey. Their stores are pleasantly laid out, but the design revolution of the past decade might never have happened. The exclamation marks, of which Sir Terence Conran is so fond as a way of signposting departments, as yet have no place in a John Lewis store. If you are lost, you ask an assistant, sorry, a partner. Sir Ralph Halpern's galleria might just as well have never been invented.

Peter Lewis explained: 'The Partnership does not believe that the larger the better, or the faster the growth the better, either for the true health of the business or for the comfort of customers. Our ambition is not size but quality. But the Partnership does generate vitality. Vitality leads to success, and over the years, little by little, that success does lead to a measurably bigger business and, always provided it is controlled and nourished, to higher standards of performance and of strength.'

The group's target audience is beautifully undefined, consisting of 'those people who can recognise and appreciate value, who want character, good taste and quality in the goods they buy.' In other words, John Lewis wants to trade with customers who want to trade with it. What it means in practice is that, while the store surroundings may be no more than functional, the emphasis is on stocking merchandise that enough people will want, at attractive prices, whether it is a bow tie, a pillow case, a towel or a kettle.

The pricing policy is summed up in the enigmatic and slightly coy slogan 'Never knowingly undersold', which was first used in Peter Jones in 1925. It is not surprising that the phrase goes over some people's heads, as 'undersold' does not appear in most versions of the Oxford English Dictionary. In plain English, the claim is that the chain never deliberately sells anything at a higher price than it can be bought for elsewhere. If the same item is on sale cheaper in another shop, Lewis will refund the difference.

'Customers are not usually expert in the merchandise they wish to buy, but rely for such knowledge on the shop that serves them,' said Peter Lewis. 'The Partnership believes that people ought to be able to rely upon their shopkeepers confidently and totally. We aim at complete candour and honesty in all our trading operations and communications with the public.'

In the late 1930s the group expanded, taking over Waitrose and Selfridges Provincial Stores. Waitrose was then a chain of ten grocers in south London. It had begun life as Waite, Rose and Taylor at the turn of the century, and was to form the basis of Waitrose supermarkets after the war. Selfridges Provincial gave the group another fifteen stores round the country, and doubled overall turnover. Now it has eighty supermarkets and 21 department stores, mainly trading under their original names like Trewin Brothers of Watford, George Henry Lee of Liverpool or Robert Sayle of Cambridge.

John Lewis appears to be adapting just as fast to the out-of-town trend. In May 1986 Peter Lewis declared: 'No out-of-town retailing in this country can compare for diversity, character and quality with modernised city centres, properly served by car parking and public transport. It is to be hoped that the planning authorities will do their utmost on the widest possible social grounds to encourage lively and rewarding inner city investments.'

But only two months later Stuart Hampson, then the newly appointed director of research and expansion, was extolling a decision to buy eight and a half acres of land at Cressex, on the outskirts of High Wycombe, immediately adjacent to the M40, for a department store carrying principally furniture and furnishings. It is due to open in 1988.

'Our continued investment in town centres shows that we firmly believe they have a strong future as the focus of shopping in this country,' said Hampson. 'There are, however, some localities where we know we would do well but where the existing town centres cannot offer a site of the size and with the car parking and access which the Partnership needs. We cannot ignore the current of change which is leading to a growth in out-of-town shopping. If there is to be a major shift in shopping patterns, the Partnership cannot be left unprepared for it.'

But if John Lewis is finally to embrace the out-of-town trend with a stand-alone site, not part of a shopping centre, then it is determined to do so in its own style. Simpler and cheaper construction methods are being used, and there will be fewer partners to the square foot.

'One of our objects in this venture is to experiment with sim-plified and therefore less expensive construction methods,' said Hampson. 'Let me hasten to say that we are not going to start trading in a "shed" and the emphasis on quality will be as much a feature of High Wycombe as it is of any of our other department stores. The poor image of some traders is a factor of their retailing standards rather than their location. The Partnership intends to show how attractive an out-of-town department store can be. There is no question of risking the Partnership's reputation for giving good service. At the same time we may wish to employ alternative shopkeeping techniques which are particularly appli-cable where space is at less of a premium than it is in a conventional city centre site. Those techniques may allow us to operate with a smaller complement of Partners in a branch of this type.'

However, the group is sticking to the conventional wisdom that fashion is strictly for the high street. It will not be sold in the Cressex outlet.

Like those who pay lip service to their local church, other retailers praise John Lewis for its unwavering adherence to its standards, envying and fearing it as a competitor. But the stan-dards are simple and no secret. They do not seem difficult to copy. So why doesn't everyone emulate this company?

It is at that point in the conversation that lesser mortals begin to look at the floor and shuffle their feet. Simple rules can be the hardest of all to follow for those not possessed of the faith, for they do not admit of compromise. Either you are for it or against it, and that goes for John Lewis' customers. Many are unaware of the partnership ethos, and there is no reason why they should be. Others seek out a Lewis branch to breathe the pure air and support what they see as a model for other commercial organisa-tions. Some, maybe a minority, avoid it for what they perceive as its atmosphere of sanctimonious smugness. But the ghost of Spe-dan, curiously akin to the BBC's Lord Reith, still stalks the counters, lifting a drape here, adjusting a price there – and daring shoppers to worship elsewhere.

MARKS & SPENCER: THE RETAILERS' RETAILER

People complain that British high streets tend to look the same, because they are becoming dominated by the big chains. But the real puzzle is that they are not filled with Marks & Spencer clones. It is the chain which every other retailer admires, envies even. Some try to copy it. They all aspire to its standards and judge their own performance against that of M & S. Yet those which have tried to come closest to an M & S style of operation, such as Littlewoods and BhS, always seem to fall short. Why?

At first blush, there seems nothing complicated about the M & S formula. They keep things as simple as possible, try to give value for money: there are no frills or gimmicks in the stores and they spend next to nothing on advertising. They do have their renowned relationship with suppliers. Marks' specifications are so tight that the company has been called a manufacturer without factories. They have been known to insist on suppliers installing canteens and making other changes that go beyond the normal remit of even the most important trade customers. However, other chains have tumbled to the importance of gaining an upper hand over manufacturers, to the extent that this has become a dominant theme of post-war retailing.

In common with the best and most durable of the other retailers, Marks has supreme self-confidence in all it does. And, like John Lewis, it has a coherent philosophy that runs through every decision, every activity.

Lord Sieff, chairman of M & S from 1972 to 1984 and now president of the company, summed it up in six rules:

1. Offer customers, under the company's brand name, St Michael, a selected range of high-quality, well-designed and attractive merchandise at reasonable prices which present good value.

2. Encourage suppliers to use the most modern and efficient techniques of production based on the latest developments in science and technology.

3. With the co-operation of suppliers, enforce high standards of quality control.

4. Wherever possible find United Kingdom sources of supply.

5. Simplify operational procedures so that the business runs reasonably efficiently.

6. Foster good human relations with staff, customers and suppliers.

However, it is one thing to sit down and dream up a business philosophy. It is quite another matter to put it into practice and make sure that it works. The key, in Marks' case, lies in the emphasis it places on human relations.

Lord Sieff said in a speech to the Institute of Directors in 1969: 'Management must care for the people they employ in all aspects of their daily work. Now I am not talking about sentimentality and "do gooders", but about care in a sensible way, which we have found brings a response, with few exceptions, from all grades of staff. This response expresses itself in loyalty to the firm, co-operation with management, greater labour stability and a willing acceptance of new and more modern methods. The majority of workers under such conditions take pride in doing a good job. All this results in greater productivity and higher profits. This enables management both to provide all those facilities which make for a contented and hard-working staff, and to pay better wages based on genuinely increased productivity. So it is of benefit to the individual, the firm and the national effort.'

But it took time to develop this caring and ultimately very profitable attitude to the workforce. M & S began a little like the company that was to become the Empire Stores mail order house, in that each was founded by a penniless immigrant who graduated from being a pedlar to renting a stall in Leeds' open market. But whereas Empire's Fattorini family quickly moved on to selling watches and silverware, Marks stayed resolutely down-market.

Marks sold socks, stockings, buttons, pins, needles and wool. Even with this simple fare he was able to lay down some of the principles upon which M & S is based today. A lot of his customers were also immigrants. A high proportion, embarrassed at their shaky grasp of English, were loath to discuss the goods on display, or ask the price. So Marks divided his stall in two. One half had items at various prices. The other half was laid out under a banner boldly declaring the now-famous slogan, 'Don't Ask The Price – It's A Penny'.

That made it easy for shoppers, and easy for Marks to keep track of his sales. Soon the whole stall was devoted to the penny price, an idea that has been widely copied. Woolworths used to sell everything under 6d (2½p), and at one time there was a Fifty-Shilling Tailor chain, selling suits at £2.50 or less.

Although M & S celebrated its centenary in 1984, taking the Penny Bazaar as its starting point, it did not become Marks & Spencer until 1894. That was when Marks went into partnership with Tom Spencer, who had been cashier for Isaac Dewhirst, the wholesaler who lent Marks £5 to start in business. The partnership did not last long. Spencer retired nine years later, at the age of 51, and Marks died four years after that, when he was only 44.

For ten years, until 1917, the fate of M & S hung in the balance. Business associates of the two founders took control, and nearly sold it. After a courtroom battle the Marks family bought sole control and Michael's son Simon became chairman when he was 28.

By then the company had expanded into more than 120 stores, plus a handful of the old market stalls. Wartime inflation had forced it to abandon the penny price, and it was under attack from Woolworths which had landed in Britain from the US in 1909. The contrasting fortunes of the two chains between then and now speaks volumes.

Like Jack Cohen of Tesco in the late 1930s, Simon Marks went to America to learn the secrets of his trade. He set sail in 1924 and later recalled: 'It was there that I learned many new things. It was about my first serious lesson in the chain store art. I learned the value of more imposing, commodious premises, modern methods of administration and the statistical control of stocks in relation to sales. I learned that new accounting machines could help to reduce the time to give the necessary information to hours instead of weeks. I learned the value of counter footage, that is, that each counter foot of space had to pay wages, rent, overhead expenses, and earn a profit. There could be no blind spots on the counters in so far as goods are concerned. This meant a much more exhaustive study of the goods we were selling and the needs of the public. It meant that the staff who were operating with me had to be re-educated and retrained. It meant new people, new forces.'

America reminded Marks to return to the idea of a price limit.

The concept had been discontinued after the penny barrier had been breached, but in the US the five and ten-cent store was commonplace – and successful. He created a new ceiling of five shillings (25p).

But the trip instilled another thought in Marks' head – one which was eventually to revolutionise retailing in Britain. He wanted to be able to interpret the customer's needs to the manufacturers. That would involve bypassing the wholesalers and giving the manufacturers direct and detailed orders, in return for which they would get guaranteed production runs.

But, strange though it sounds today, M & S had a credibility problem. Aside from the wholesalers' opposition, they had an uphill struggle to persuade manufacturers to do business with a chain still best known for penny bazaars. And they had to invent their own brand name, because the suppliers were not going to put their own name to goods which had been specified by a retailer. St Michael was chosen in memory of Michael Marks, and because he was the guardian angel of the Jewish people. Nowadays suppliers beg to be allowed to put their name under St Michael on the labels. They are always refused. No other brand is permitted in an M & S store.

That policy determined the type of goods M & S was prepared to sell. They had to be reliable, repeatable, improvable and open to cost reductions as efficiency increased. Hence the concentration on textiles and food, which has only gradually been widened again to include things like plants, books and china.

This approach has been likened to that of a Japanese corporation. It strikes fear in M & S's rivals, because it often means that the company takes a long time to digest a new idea before putting it into practice in its own formidable way. The introduction of the Chargecard followed this pattern. M & S was late into in-store cards and studied the market very carefully indeed. When it moved, it moved decisively. Within two years it had a million cardholders, and has put that list of core customers to good use. On the reasonable assumption that they are more affluent and more committed to the group than most of its customers, M & S invites them to special evening events where they can shop, express their opinions and say what goods they would like to see on sale. M & S has subsequently been granted a deposit-taking licence by the Bank of England, because cardholders who return garments have their account credited, so they are often in surplus. Once there are three million cardholders there will be a big enough base to start selling them insurance and other financial services.

Not all the policy initiatives have been without problems, however much advance research has been devoted to them. Both of the group's overseas expansions, into Europe and North America, have been fraught with difficulties. They seemed natural extensions of M & S's home base. Canada shares cultural roots with Britain and a high proportion of first or second generation immigrants are familiar with the Marks & Spencer style. Many Parisians pop into the Marble Arch branch of the chain on trips to London – and, once home, pass the word round about the bargains they snapped up.

But M & S found that it was not quite as simple as that when they set up shop in those countries. The French demanded and got fitting rooms, something the chain had conceded only in its most remote UK stores. The Canadians complained that the branches were like hospital wards and wanted more casual wear. It has been a slow learning process, but by 1987 the company was feeling confident enough to strike out across the Canadian border into New York State. The Big Apple beckoned and presented M & S with its biggest challenge yet: to crack the notoriously fickle US retail market. 'We think we have something different to offer the Americans,' said marketing executive Ronnie Jacobson.

Back in the UK, the group has come under a degree of criticism for allegedly being left behind by the high street's design revolution. In tones of reproachfulness the chain has been accused of becoming dowdy and utilitarian, lacking in imagination and flair.

Harsh words, which echoed round the ears of Lord Rayner when he took over as chairman in 1984, the first from outside the founding families to do so since the interregnum between Michael and Simon Marks in the early years of the century.

Looking back, Rayner said: 'We had to update the appearance of our stores We needed new methods, a new approach to presenting goods, retraining of staff to work in this different environment, plus the sums of money to bring it all about. The high streets are changing. The whole world is becoming more conscious of leisure, thus clothing for leisure is becoming more important. We had to get to grips with the development of casual wear. Also, people spend more time at home because of central heating, TV, video, drinks in the home. So we are using our skills in design, style, looks and co-ordination. People like to know they can buy matching goods.'

He reinforced this change of tack by ordering £1.5 billion to be spent on modernising and improving the stores. Apart from its presence in out-of-town shopping centres, the group is cautiously moving into stand-alone sites in tandem with Tesco and Asda, and opening satellite stores for individual departments. These have sprung out of opportunism. There is not enough room to expand in and around many of its normal stores, so satellites are being opened within a few minutes' walk, under the charge of the same manager.

That is the sort of opportunism that Marks has not demonstrated for years. All the signs are that the group is in the throes of one of its periodic leaps forward, cashing in on its immense fund of goodwill with a shopping population that had perhaps begun to take it for granted.

But it is happening within the framework of the philosophy laid down by Michael Marks and his descendants. The present team, under Rayner, are too well trained to want to overthrow their inheritance. But they realise that retailing has become a much tougher and more competitive business. That is reflected in a more flexible and pragmatic attitude, which they expect their suppliers to share. Reactions are quicker. And that can only mean one thing for the rest of the high street: the old penny bazaar is limbering up to become an even more formidable foe.

Supermarkets:
The Dinosaurs of the
21st Century

THE PROTAGONISTS:
- *J. SAINSBURY*
- *TESCO*

Supermarkets have been the all-conquering heroes of the retail revolution. From their introduction into Britain after the Second World War, everything they have touched has seemingly turned to gold for their owners. Little did the humdrum grocers at the end of the last century realise that their successors would become unimaginably rich – and all for driving to its logical conclusion the simple aim of bringing customers the widest choice at the lowest prices.

But as the next century beckons it may be that the tide is about to turn away from supermarkets, leaving them on the edge of town like so many beached whales surrounded by their vast, echoing car parks. Rising standards of living and a rapidly changing age profile may cut the numbers of people willing to undergo a combination of the Monte Carlo rally and one of those games where mice are trained to run up and down as many alleyways as possible before reaching the cheese – or, in the case of supermarkets, the checkouts – in the shortest possible time.

It has a gruesome novelty value, but like the dinosaurs the seed of the supermarkets' extinction in their present form may lie in their very success. The traffic congestion in the car parks of the bigger superstores, as they are called, is matched only by the trolley congestion inside the stores. Just as wider roads seem to produce more snarl-ups, so wider aisles appear to attract trolley jams.

And for what? A brief brush with a heady new aspirational lifestyle? A chance to buy smoked salmon along with the baked beans? The supermarkets have done much to tickle our palates and add a bit of fun to what for many is a chore. But will we always be willing to put up with the chore? The public has made it plain that it does not like struggling with a week's groceries in and out of the lift of a multi-storey car park, which in any case can be dingy and even dangerous after dark. So flat, open parks are the rule. The public wanted wider aisles, better lighting, less canned music. They got them. But what happens if an ageing and affluent public decides it is fed up climbing into a car and battling through crowds? The supermarketeers will have to respond again, and yet more radically.

That way lies home shopping, perusing the choices on video tapes and making selections by computer. The stores can be turned into warehouses, the car parks into lorry bays. The only element that cannot be varied in the foreseeable future is food and drink's sheer bulk. The rest is up for grabs, open to debate, exposed to changing fashion. The big supermarket groups like to talk about how they are introducing more convenience and pleasure into grocery shopping. They are indeed, but what they have done is really only tinker around the edges, updating and refining the basic arrangement that has existed since farmers brought their produce to market so that shoppers could take that produce home.

The street markets shrank as methods of distribution improved and specialist food retailers set themselves up in the high street. The evolutionary process was stunted for a while by Resale Price Maintenance, which allowed manufacturers to tell retailers what to charge the public in the name of preserving the makers' muscle and the bank balances of the corner shop. It was a device to divide and rule. But they reckoned without the likes of Jack Cohen.

Cohen was a street trader who graduated to the high street but never left his instincts behind. When Bex Bissel, the carpet shampoo firm, insisted he charge the prices they set he blew the whistle on them by posting a notice outside his shop informing customers that they would have to pay £1 more than he wanted them to pay because the manufacturer said so!

That was in 1961. It was one of the last battles of a thirty' years war. Resale Price Maintenance was outlawed three years later, in the teeth of opposition from manufacturers and the corner shop lobby. Some of their fears have come to pass. Tesco and Sainsbury alone account for nearly a third of the grocery market, and the small shopkeeper has had to make a living from emergency and specialist needs, often by staying open longer hours.

But the revolution that took everyone by surprise was the switch to self-service. Conventional wisdom stated that the British public preferred counter service, and besides it would be an open invitation to pilfering if shoppers were permitted to take things off the shelves. At first the die-hards seemed to be right. Early experiments were erratic. Post-war rationing did not help, for customers still had to go to a separate desk to have their coupons checked, and the restrictions imposed by war and its aftermath militated against innovation and enterprise on the consumer front.

But those who could afford to cross the Atlantic had seen the future, and it worked. Supermarkets had sprung up in the United States in the 1930s, driven by the Depression to find ways of getting cheap food to people whose living standards were slipping monthly. Unfettered competition, inexpensive land and an absence of planning restrictions set off an explosion. Atlantic & Pacific, the then leader, had 3,500 supermarkets by 1947.

The new concept offered a glittering prospect. Labour costs were slashed, the overwhelming majority of people did not after all try to stuff groceries in their pockets and the open displays tempted them to buy goodies on impulse as well as the standard list of items they originally came for.

The best of the British supermarket groups claim that they have overtaken the expertise of the American pioneers, in terms of product development, innovation, and warehousing back-up. The US chains may disagree, but the fact is that they can open a store for £5 million, whereas the equivalent costs £25 million on a typical UK site. That concentrates the mind like nothing else in business.

On the other hand, the British chains have an advantage that they do not usually like to admit. While they chafe against planning restrictions, it is ultimately to their advantage that local authorities will not allow two superstores next to one another, as happens in the US. That gives a new UK store a clear chance to pay its way, yet the car-borne shopper can normally expect to have an alternative within a convenient distance.

The car has allowed the different types of bulk shopping, from food to furniture, to move out of town, leaving the high street free for the pedestrian to roam up and down comparing clothes, jewellery, financial services and other 'lightweight' offerings.

Mind you, supermarket proprietors are quite happy to shift out of the comparison league whenever possible. The difficulty of making detailed comparisons between out-of-town superstores has given them the opportunity to orchestrate their prices more cunningly – and they do. They all pay lip service to price, especially in newspaper advertisements. But they know that, once shoppers have the confidence to visit a particular store in the knowledge that prices will be generally competitive, it is fairly easy to lure them upmarket into the tempting exotica and luxuries. Even if they do notice the odd few pence more on a certain item, it will hardly be worth making an extra journey for such a small saving. When they get in the store they want it to be clean and pleasant, and to have things like a 'live' bakery, a delicatessen and a good wine and spirits selection, just to liven up the bare necessities of life. Avowedly 'healthy' food has sold like hot cakes since early 1985, and labelling is more informative.

A survey by the Consumers' Association in 1982 showed that more than half the sample used large stores for the bulk of their grocery shopping, and seven out of ten shopped once a week in a single store. It is no wonder that, in retrospect at least, the rise and rise of the supermarket seems so inevitable.

The challenge for the supermarkets is to cater for improved standards of living and increased leisure time. People can eat and drink only so much, but that does not mean that they cannot eat better, nor that they want to spend anything like as much time on preparing what they buy.

Marks & Spencer, as it does so often, led the way a decade ago when it turned traditional thinking on its head by starting off with high-quality ready-made meals like kebabs, and only gradually moving on to routine commodities. It also exerted its famed influence on manufacturers to make exactly what it wanted to sell, and not merely what the manufacturers wanted to supply. M & S was in a very strong position to do that because of its policy of selling only goods bearing its own St Michael label. Like John Lewis's Waitrose supermarket chain, Marks was able to make use of the enormous goodwill already surrounding its name to per-suade the public to buy food from it. The orthodox supermarket chains have been working hard to generate goodwill of their own on a similar scale, and some have succeeded. The pressures imposed by an increasingly sophisticated public in a static market will ensure that they will need every ounce of that goodwill to overcome the next generation of obstacles and opportunities.

THE MIDDLE CLASSES' FAVOURITE GROCER

J. Sainsbury vies with Waitrose, the John Lewis subsidiary, as the southern middle classes' idea of what a supermarket should be like

– good, healthy provisions at low prices, tastefully presented. The image is personified by the family's latest chairman, Sir John, a bluff and beaming six-footer. He is a great-grandson of the founder, John James Sainsbury, who married the daughter of a north London dairyman and opened a dairy in 1869 at 178 Drury Lane. After Stowe and Oxford, Sir John went straight into the family business, becoming a director eight years later at the age of 31. His cousin, David, is finance director of the company and his brothers, Timothy and Simon, were on the board. Sir John and David between them personally own 220 million shares in the company worth over £800 million, but they give their entire dividends to charity. In 1986 those dividends were worth £12 million before tax. That is entirely consistent with the declared Sainsbury aim to behave to the highest standards with complete integrity, contributing to the public good and to the quality of life in the community. Virtue may well have its own reward, but virtue in retailing is often rewarded more tangibly.

If a customer does not like a shop, especially a grocer's, he or she does not have to go back. Conversely, if a shop does well there is soon enough profit to open another, and then another. Once there is enough trade to cover overheads, the profit on every extra pound spent goes straight into the owner's pocket – or can be ploughed into expanding the business. John James Sainsbury was brought up in Lambeth, one of London's poorer districts, and his ambition was to be able to afford to open a branch of the dairy for each of his sons. His wife bore twelve children, of whom six were boys, but the growth of the business soon outstripped the size of even that family.

Yet the company, which by 1986 was operating more than 800 outlets of different kinds, seems to have found it easier than some of its Victorian contemporaries to change with the times and stay ahead of the competition. John James's dying words were said to have been 'keep the shops well lit'. Lord Sainsbury, now the group's joint president, elaborated on that simple dictum: 'In my opinion the firms that are successful in retailing are those which adjust to changing social circumstances. In our case we saw those as first, a rising standard of living; second, mobility, with more and more families having motor cars; and third, the factor of domestic refrigeration – the ordinary fridge to begin with, and then the freezer.'

He was explaining what was probably the company's most controversial decision, to convert from its traditional long marble-topped counters into self-service. In 1949 Lord (then Alan) Sainsbury and a colleague toured the supermarkets of the United States, an idea put to them by the British Ministry of Food, and returned convinced. Their next task was to convince their customers, some of whom appeared to regret the passing of an era with considerable vigour. The first Sainsbury's supermarket opened in Croydon the following year, to the sounds of abuse from irate shoppers and a wire basket aimed at the chairman's head.

Happily, other shoppers took a more charitable view of the new style of trading, and the concept soon established itself in the high street. Yet had the company not taken that decision, there is little doubt that it would soon have been left behind as one of food retailing's backwaters. Sainsbury has since spent hundreds of millions of pounds to keep up with each new expansion of the supermarket concept, though it did not close the last counter store until 1982.

The average store today is only ten years old, and over forty per cent of the group's selling space has been opened within the last five years. They have to have plenty of parking space, usually for around 500 cars at each store being built now. Aisles have grown wider, partly for greater comfort but also because people buy more per visit and so need bigger trolleys. A family of four trundles out with about 80 lb of weekly necessities these days.

But the biggest change, at Sainsbury as with every other supermarket group, has been in the range of goods on show. The modest 500 lines available in 1950 have swollen to 10,000 today. A third of those are sold under Sainsbury's own label, varying in the company's own words 'from cornflakes to Cheddar, from claret to capsicums and from cake to cosmetics'. Sainsbury is the UK's largest retailer of wine, meat and fresh fruit and vegetables.

Tom Vyner, the assistant managing director in charge of buying and marketing, explained: 'We stock a store according to its size and environment. You fill the store according to its capacity to stock the range. Our priority is to serve the customer as best we can, and we reckon to fill it with a range we can keep stocked throughout the year.' Only 120 Sainsbury's are big enough to stock the entire range, but that number is growing all the time.

'Fridges give shoppers more storage for perishable goods,'

pointed out Joe Barnes, the assistant managing director responsible for retailing, 'and there is more leisure time. Eating has changed from a ritual to a chore. You can prepare a meal in five minutes flat with a microwave, because people prefer more time for other things. And it's not just that they can afford a microwave: now they have greater access to credit.'

These social changes have been duly reflected in Sainsbury's sales pattern. There are more luxury goods going through the checkouts, and an enormous growth in wine. Preserves and pastes are declining, perhaps because they are bought more frequently as part of ready-prepared meals, and as more and more technology infiltrates the business of food preservation.

A striking example of the speed of change is the contrast between Sainsbury's Cowley branch, built in 1962 and refurbished in 1978, and the newly-built store in nearby Heyford Hill, Oxford, only a mile and a half away.

Just as department stores increasingly put their perfume section by the front door to create interest as shoppers come in, so Heyford Hill greets customers with an enormous produce department at the front of the new store, which is an idea others are following. The consumer can make his or her own quality selection. They no longer have to run the risk of rotten grapes or bruised tomatoes. So the fresh food has to be of pristine quality, or it will still be sitting there at the end of the day.

The floor area at Heyford Hill is more than half as big again as Cowley, which means that aisles can be wider and shelves lower. That gives more room for the bigger trolleys and makes the store less claustrophobic, especially for women. The mood is automatically more relaxed, and people are more inclined to buy, and to experiment with new types of food and drink, the types that often carry higher profit margins.

The refrigeration is more open now. When the Cowley store was being built the fridge was all-important. Now air cooling is the order of the day. That makes the shelves easier to fill, easier to display and so easier to sell from. Consequently the ratio of frozen to chilled food has changed. As technology has improved in this area, so there is much more chilled food, which is more appealing than frozen. That has paved the way for more gourmet items, like smoked salmon and shellfish. And to wash down such exotica, the size and range of the wine department have increased enormously.

An in-store bakery, fish counter and delicatessen are now standard. 'Our research showed that supermarkets had become somewhat impersonal,' said Barnes. 'The fish, delicatessen and bakery counters help to overcome that, and now we have these different departments, with someone there to help the customer in each one. It's a question of human contact. We have the most intense trading of any supermarket group, and we fill most of the shop when it's closed, so that there is enough on the shelves when it is trading.'

Heating technology has improved to the point where Sainsbury no longer needs built-in heating in the new stores. It all comes from the refrigeration, by turning round the heat which is extracted from those units. And the light fittings double as air extractors, the whole system being computer controlled.

Sainsbury claims to have advanced further into the computer age than any of its competitors, both in terms of stock control and checkout facilities.

'The customer expects to be processed as fast and accurately as possible,' said Barnes. 'The great majority of our stores will have scanning checkouts by 1988. To carry the benefit through, you then have to provide a packing service, because the goods are read automatically but they still have to be packed by hand. The technology exists to scan a whole trolley, but it is expensive and is still at the purely laboratory, prototype stage. That is for the 2000s.'

Those same electronic messages are relayed to the stock room and the distribution depots to report which shelves need refilling, and which goods need reordering. The next step is to plug the computers through to the suppliers, to start the lorries rolling before the gaps appear in the warehouses.

But in one high-tech area Sainsbury remains deliberately cautious: credit cards. Said Vyner: 'On the research and experiments we have carried out, the vast majority of people do not want to use credit cards to buy food. They do not want to build a credit liability for food. No food retailer in the US takes them, and they are far more credit-card conscious than we are, as a nation. The two supermarket groups who do use them have a high non-food element. We take them on non-food in the hypermarkets and the Homebase DIY.'

Although this time it is a question of commercial judgement

rather than ethical principle, that caution recalls echoes of another famous rearguard action by Sainsbury in the 1960s, when it fought almost singlehandedly against trading stamps being 'given away' with groceries, arguing that the public would prefer lower prices. They did, and the competition eventually had to abandon stamps to keep prices down. That battle may have to be fought all over again, as Richard Tompkins is reviving his Green Shield Stamps. But it will be interesting to see if Sainsbury can win a similar victory on credit cards, as the British seem to be getting less worried about buying on credit and supermarket bills never seem to shrink. They say they are keeping an open mind on the problem.

Sainsbury is gradually moving its centre of gravity out of town, helped by its Homebase DIY and garden centre chain, and its joint venture with BhS into SavaCentre, which combines super-market shopping with BhS's clothing, household and electrical goods, car accessories, toys, books and stationery. To that extent some see it as a risky venture.

Conventional retailing wisdom states that clothing is a com-parison item, that customers like to walk up and down the high street comparing rival offerings rather than get in a car and commit themselves to one store isolated from its competitors. The risk is partly Sainsbury's because it is run by a separate company owned 50:50 by the partners. They do not just take out the profits from their own activities, but share in one another's success or otherwise. Both sides express themselves content with the ven-ture, which has encouraged Tesco and Marks & Spencer to try their hand at something similar, though crucially different in that they are operating on a shared site but in separate buildings. SavaCentre's biggest limitation has been the problem of finding sites and getting permission to develop them, so only six were started between 1977 and 1986.

'The high street will continue, but people no longer make frequent trips to the small supermarket,' said Joe Barnes. 'We can be interested in being just off the high street. We have to be able to put the 1990 sort of facilities in the store, we have to be able to deliver conveniently to the store and there has to be enough car parking. Take Chiswick: we are fifty yards behind the high street, but with the ability to deliver and with pedestrian access. There is a fine distinction between out of town and edge of town. It doesn't affect our approach, but most 1990s stores are edge of town. Out of town generates interest, commercial assessment, other businesses, and local housing to house the workers employed in those new businesses. So it becomes edge of town.'

The next campaign is to extend the supermarkets' opening hours, so that people can buy what they want when they want, within reason. So Sainsbury chips away at the permitted hours little by little. 'Without any legal restriction, we would like to be open 8 'til 8 on Monday, Tuesday and Wednesday, and 8 'til 10 on Thursday, Friday and, in some stores, on Saturday,' said Barnes. Many local authorities resist such liberalisation, with an eye on the interests of local residents and local small shopkeepers. But so far the tide has been moving in only one direction, and that is likely to continue.

Sainsbury, thanks largely to its ruling family's refusal to compromise its standards or shorten its aims, has evolved a strategy which appears to be timeless. It has taken the classic management textbook path of keeping the business as simple as possible – giving the customers what they want in attractive surroundings at competitive prices – and in so doing building a relationship of trust and loyalty with generations of shoppers. However, the group has been fortunate in being taken into the supermarket era by two extremely shrewd and far-seeing chairmen, Lord Sainsbury and his son Sir John. The long-term test will be to see how it survives their passing.

GOODBYE TO 'PILE IT HIGH, SELL IT CHEAP'

Tesco is the store that nearly died. One of the retailing success stories of the immediate post-war era, the company was almost fatally slow to respond to the changes in public taste that began in the 1960s. While the late Sir John Cohen, the group's brilliant founder, and his sons-in-law, Hyman Kreitman and Sir Leslie Porter, were still filling their supermarkets from floor to ceiling with the essentials at the lowest prices, the public was slowly but surely moving on to demand better quality, wider choice, more luxuries and the opportunity to buy a different lifestyle.

When he arrived in the high street, Jack Cohen applied a street trader's techniques to food retailing. He had started in street markets in the Hackney and Hammersmith districts of London after the First World War. He bought supplies wherever he could, often substandard goods or stock from a factory that was being shut down, and auctioned them to the customers.

In 1930 Cohen took his auctions into covered markets. His first were called Bargain Centres of London, but gradually he introduced the Tesco name, which had originally been a brand of tea Cohen sold. The name was a combination of the intitials of T. E. Stockwell, the tea merchant he bought from, and the first two letters of his own name.

By 1932 Cohen realised that the auction method meant he was missing chances to sell regular groceries. He was pulling in the shoppers, but was not selling all the things they wanted to buy. So he moved on to more conventional trading, with two huge pyramids of cans at the front of the shop and a counter at the back. Orthodoxy brought him up against the big manufacturers, who in many cases took steps to ensure that he was charging the prices they laid down.

It was to be more than thirty years before that battle was won, and Resale Price Maintenance was abolished. In the meantime Cohen discovered supermarkets, which were much more akin to street trading than the straightforward grocery shop.

In 1935 he was a big enough customer of American suppliers such as Heinz, Libby and Del Monte for him to be invited to the US to see their operations. And that was when he saw the forerunners of today's supermarkets. They were open-air, roadside affairs, but the basic principle was there. Shoppers were quite prepared to pick what they wanted and pay as they left.

Four years later, Cohen was back in the US. Supermarkets had taken off. This time they were in converted warehouses and waste ground. What they lacked in site appeal they made up in brash publicity, and people were filling their cars with piles of merchandise. Cohen recalled: 'It was astonishing. In such a short space of years, self-service shopping had moved into what looked like the big league and the competitive effect was obvious to even the casual visitor like myself, when hordes of people milled around these places. I could not help wondering about conducting an experiment in England. Unfortunately, the war intervened and I had to wait many years before I took the plunge.'

He started fitfully, with a store at 67a St Peter's Street, St Albans, Hertfordshire, in 1947. The customers were cautious, and the paraphernalia of rationing gummed the self-service idea. The experiment was ended after less than a year. But Tesco also went public in 1947, which gave the group extra resources. Cohen reopened the St Albans store with a more streamlined system, and as rationing was dismantled and wages began to rise, supermarkets carved out their corner of the high street.

Tesco expanded to the point where it had a nationwide chain of more than 700 stores by the mid-1960s, and Cohen was a multimillionaire knighted for his services to retailing. But like many other businesses before and since, Tesco fell victim to its founder's vision. Ian MacLaurin, the present chairman of the group, explained: 'Within ten years of achieving national coverage, the future of the entire company was at risk. The City was writing us down, the company's market share was falling, and Tesco's image with the public was at zero.' It was a dramatic turnround which called for drastic action to halt the slide.

Aside from the crowded layout of Tesco's supermarkets and the mix of goods on offer, one of the biggest bones of contention was its policy of giving trading stamps to customers. They had been introduced, amid considerable controversy, in 1963 as a way of getting round the laws on Resale Price Maintenance. Tesco had been taken to court for selling goods at less than the price laid down by the manufacturer, but manufacturers could hardly argue if a shop chose to give something away at the checkout.

The idea was that shoppers collected the stamps in books which they could exchange for goods at shops run by the stamp companies. They were an obvious come-on, but there was an equally obvious snag for the retailers: if every chain gave stamps the competitive advantage would be wiped out and the only gainers would be the stamp companies. So the National Association of Multiple Grocers, which Tesco belonged to, agreed to ban them. But Fine Fare broke that ban, and most of the other big chains soon followed suit. Sainsbury significantly stood aloof.

Tesco entered the fray with Cohen's usual gusto, becoming a leader of the stamps war. But, ironically, within a couple of years of the campaign taking off its rationale disappeared. Resale Price Maintenance was abolished, so retailers could charge what prices they liked and thereby assert their power over the suppliers. For a time Tesco tried to have it both ways – stamps and lowest prices – but inevitably the stampless supermarkets had an unavoidable edge which Sainsbury used to capitalise on its growing reputation for quality. They did not have to pay the stamp companies two per cent of turnover, a vital advantage in a business which normally works on profit margins of only four or five per cent.

Tesco began to slip in the supermarket league table, just as the leadership of the company was going through transition. Cohen claimed: 'We feel we have the best know-how of self-service methods, and this has come from an attitude of mind on the part of the management team: that they really believe they are the best.' But MacLaurin, who was at that stage making his way up the management ladder, said: 'It was a family business, and Jack couldn't stand accountants. Having achieved its own self-imposed targets in the 1960s, Tesco assumed that its future was secure. But it came through strongly in the 1970s that we were going no place. It was crisis management. Decisions were taken and untaken by the week. We needed a strategy and the guts to go through with it.'

The upshot was a boardroom battle over whether Tesco should continue with trading stamps. MacLaurin led the fight against them. He won and in 1977 put his name to Operation Checkout, which marked the end of Tesco's stamp era and the beginning of an out-and-out price war. That campaign took Tesco's share of the grocery market up from seven per cent to twelve per cent within a year, and MacLaurin's name was made within the organisation.

But nearly doubling turnover in such a short space brought its own problems. The capacity of the stores and their warehouses was stretched to the limit. That forced Tesco to make a strategic decision – whether to press on with the 'pile it high, sell it cheap' policy or to move upmarket.

MacLaurin explained: 'Jack Cohen was a great retailer, flying by the seat of his pants, with a fantastic feel for trading. But then we lost our way. Public aspirations started to change. Tesco did not really make it in the modern shopping idiom of the mid-1970s.' So MacLaurin took the chain upmarket.

It took a while for the change in strategy to make itself felt, for it involved a change in the nature of the stores themselves. The group had to go for bigger sites, which gave it the scope to offer better lighting, wider aisles and a more comfortable environment. But that meant taking one step back for every two steps forward. In the past decade Tesco has cut the number of stores from 850 to 340, but the total sales area has risen by half, reflecting the transition from 4,000 sq ft high street supermarkets to the new 65,000 sq ft superstores, of which it has more than 100.

MacLaurin, a still-young and determined careerist, started his Tesco career on a cricket ground at Eastbourne. Jack Cohen was one of the spectators. He met the teams afterwards and offered any of the players a job if they wanted one. MacLaurin, then in junior management, went for an interview. He remembered: 'Jack said "What are you earning?" I told him £900 a year. He said, "All right, I'll pay you £900 a year for six months, then if we like one another I'll pay you £1,000 a year plus a car." Having a car was a great attraction, so I took the job.' By the time he went full-time into the Tesco management he had been loading vans, buying meat and vegetables, and running stores. There is not an aspect of the company he has not been involved in, and that is a tradition handed straight down from Jack Cohen.

Now he is concentrating on refining the mainstream retail operation through a development programme running at £300 million a year. Ten years ago the group gave store managers considerable autonomy in buying policy. But now everything is controlled from the head office in Cheshunt, north of London. The managers are now mainly concerned with personnel. They can ask the commercial director at Cheshunt to make a modification in the range of goods on offer if there is an unexpected local demand, but that is as far as it goes these days.

Because of the more rapidly changing complexion of the population in Britain, when Tesco is designing a store the ethnic mix and its particular needs is one of the first elements it re-searches, along with disposable income, traffic patterns, and the communities within reach of the new location.

'We have the UK on a computer grid,' MacLaurin explained. 'We grade the stores in size from A to H. We know the buying power of each area. We know the disposable income, we know in each case exactly what our share of the market will be, and therefore how much we should pay for the site. We know the sales per linear foot at each store. We take a decision whether to be on the high street or out of town as we go along, depending on the local conditions. It's all done to a formula. In the old days it was a question of sticking a finger in the air. There is no evidence that taking food shopping out of town destroys the high street because it takes away bulk shopping and allows comparison shopping.'

In recent years Tesco has been experimenting with the idea of letting space in its bigger stores to other retailers such as Midland Bank and Thomas Cook. But now MacLaurin feels that the company can make better use of the space itself, partly because the concessions have not been a wild success. When people go into a supermarket, it seems, they are geared up to collect the groceries and get through the checkout. Banks and travel agents are closer to comparison shopping, so there is a culture clash. The cash service of a bank is valuable, but that can be provided more economically with a hole-in-the-wall machine.

Like Sainsbury, Tesco has linked up with a non-food retailer to develop mini shopping centres with shared parking facilities. It is a richly plumed feather in Tesco's cap that its partner is Marks & Spencer, which guards its name as jealously as any retailer and would have had its pick of supermarket partners. Their first joint venture is Brookfield, near Cheshunt, with a total sales area of 100,000 sq ft. But MacLaurin rejects the SavaCentre concept, in which Sainsbury and BhS combine under one roof. 'We have had experience of two retail companies under one roof,' he said, 'and I do not think it works.'

MacLaurin makes no attempt to disguise the fact that his immediate ambition is to overtake Sainsbury's annual sales. His policies are coming through strongly now, but every time Tesco announces another surge in turnover Sainsbury somehow manages to trump it. The struggle can be nothing but good news for the consumer. 'In five years' time we should be a much stronger operator in the UK,' MacLaurin claimed. 'Beyond that, it's a question of whether we go for a major UK takeover or foreign expansion. We are getting towards maturity now, but retailing is a continuously revolving business. You never arrive. It's a restless industry, and we are all competing for a bigger slice of a static cake.'

The Chain Gangs

THE PROTAGONISTS:
- *SEARS*
- *HARRIS QUEENSWAY*
- *DIXONS*

A lot of people think that a retail product is something you can buy in a shop. But to the professionals, it is the shop itself. Because before you will go in and buy, you have to be convinced that you can trust a particular shop, that it will give you a good deal without your having to keep your wits about you, and that it is the sort of shop you are not going to be ashamed being seen coming out of. All of this adds up to a retail product, and the chains do it most skilfully of all. While a department store projects itself through sheer size, range and even opulence, the chain store group has to come up with a formula that is going to be as popular in Aberdeen as it is in Exeter, yet as distinctive in Canterbury as it is in Cumbria.

Almost every large retail company has to organise itself into chains these days, to reap the benefits of bulk buying 'umbrella' advertising campaigns. But some groups have refined the chain store philosophy into a fine art, keeping the same sites but changing the scenery according to the shifting moods of the high street and its walk-on players – the customers.

Chains were originally a way for a successful store to capitalise on its success. If shoppers in one part of town liked a certain ambience and mix of goods, then the odds were that the shoppers in a similar district a few miles away would be just as enthusiastic. The new shop could be decorated in the same way as the old, and the early retailing entrepreneurs soon realised that they could train managers to replicate the day-to-day management skills. The fact that a retailer can literally branch out into new outlets implies reliability and substance, and every additional branch acts as a permanent advertisement for the chain as a whole.

So successful were the pre-war chains that some feared that they would be shackled by law. The old butcher's, baker's, draper's and tailor's shops were driven out of business in their dozens by the new multiples selling food and clothing at far lower prices, bringing a lot of goods within poorer people's reach for the first time. The small-trader lobby reacted. A proposal was floated to limit the size of multiple chains. The mere threat was enough to throw the multiples into even more frenetic expansion, opening new outlets as fast as they were able in case the clamp came down. It never did, and the public showed that by and large it preferred the mass-produced and serviceable item to the handmade, impossibly dear alternative.

Of course, the retailer who goes in for chains must give up any notion of exclusivity, except on the most limited scale, but the potential profits from mass-marketing are far greater than from the occasional expensive sale to the wealthy few. And by developing a series of chains a retailer can target his markets more precisely. Crudely, he can develop an upmarket and a downmarket version of his basic business. In women's fashions, French Connection begat the one-off designs of Nicole Fahri, while Harris Queensway sells cheaper carpets through Mad Max. It also gives an opportunity to diversify, as the Cecil Gee menswear chain did with its Gee 2 shops for the now-fashionable casual wear. W H Smith has spread into Our Price, Paperchase and Do It All.

A number of other retailers believe that they have discovered enough of the secrets of their trade to apply them to selling anything through a shop. But there is an obvious danger of being picked off by the leaders in each sector, because of their specialist knowledge. Stanley Kalms, chairman of Dixons, and Sir Phil Harris of Harris Queensway are both confident that there is nothing beyond their reach. Both, however, are aware of the pitfalls of overconfidence. Harris claims he would not go near the fashion business, while Kalms is wary of trying to juggle too many high street brands.

If, as they and some of their rivals argue, a top-class retailing operation has to be tightly controlled, then in theory there should be a limit on the number of chains one group can run, and on the number of branches that can form a chain, without the whole business collapsing under the weight of weak links.

Woolworth's new management decided to pull back from a chain which at one time amounted to nearly 1,000 branches, of which arguably not many more than 100 were making a profit. Tesco has trimmed from 850 small stores to 340 mainly big ones, increasing its total selling area in the process. Yet McDonald's wants to expand from its current 240 outlets in Britain to more than 1,000, which will by then be part of a worldwide network of well over 10,000.

Supermarkets and variety stores may seem very different animals from hamburger bars, but it is a moot point which has the harder task. McDonald's certainly has a much smaller range of stock for its deliberately restricted menu, but it does take a risk not shared by the others to any significant extent. It finishes the manufacturing process on the premises, by cooking the food. That creates room for that many more mistakes and wastage. Because the food is cooked to be eaten while it is still warm it has to be sold in just the right condition, unlike a piece of cheese or a bag of sweets.

The reason for McDonald's success at running such a huge chain, and making them all as alike as possible, appears to lie in central staff training and controls, and this is something that the UK chain stores have latched on to only in comparatively recent years. The tradition was to give branch managers considerable autonomy within the overall framework that had been laid down. In many cases they were allowed to pursue their own buying policies and develop their own relationships with suppliers. Discipline was supposed to operate through the monthly returns the managers had to submit, and the bonuses they would receive for increased profits. But in a really big chain it was impossible to keep tabs on every manager, and some inevitably succumbed to kickbacks from unscrupulous suppliers. Central buying minimises such leaks, in return for making the branches just that shade slower to respond to changes in local taste and demand.

Cosiness can work in the other direction, too – from the manager to his or her staff. That is why several of the more successful chains make a point of switching their managers around from branch to branch. It keeps the staff on their toes, and keeps the more ambitious managers' eyes on their sales targets.

In these ways the modern chains have become more truly chain-like than their predecessors, which at times were more akin to a collection of individually-run shops that happened to share a common frontage. Central control may give the managers less job satisfaction, because often their only remaining real area of discretion is recruitment, but that is compensated for by incomes far in excess of those that could have been dreamed of by previous generations of shopkeepers.

Computerisation and market research have taken most of the guesswork and some of the inspiration out of the multiple chains. But the scope and the pressure for new ideas is as strong as ever. Sears, the number one in shoe chains, is coming under attack from Next, which is busily spawning spin-off versions of itself to make the most of its name. W H Smith had to buy Our Price because its lusty young competitor was too successful. The clothing chains, for both men and women, come and go with the fashions. The point is that, win or lose, the stakes are multiplied for the chains by every extra branch. And it is remarkably difficult to revive a chain that hits the slide. Sir Terence Conran ruthlessly chopped his Now chain once it failed to take off. The Fifty Shilling Tailors, Weaver to Wearer, Hepworth, Lipton, Pricerite, Timothy White and Taylor, Martins and Williams & Glyn's banks, all are names that have been squeezed out of the high street and consigned to the scrap heap.

FROM MANFIELD TO MAPPIN & WEBB

Sears is the silent giant that for years bestrode the high street unknown to the public – unless you were in the trade or had invested in its shares. The group has no fewer than 6000 outlets round the world. In Britain it ranges from Saxone to Garrard, the Crown jewellers, taking in Selfridges and the New Lewis's department stores as well as William Hill, the bookmaker. It is by far Britain's biggest shoe retailer.

Sears – no connection with Sears Roebuck of the US – constantly rings the changes on its portfolio of high street names to keep up with the shifts in public taste. Its latest stroke has been for the first time to use its own name, originally that of a shoe manufacturer who bought shops to give it outlets. At the Metro Centre in Gateshead the group has opened the first Sears store as a showcase for some of its leading high street names.

Its greatest success of the 1980s has been Olympus Sports, which Sears bought as a minor business for £500,000 in 1978. The timing enabled the group to take hold of the trend towards fitness fashion and spin it on to a new and more challenging retail style. Its main store in Oxford Street, London, is claimed to be the biggest sports shop in the world, and its use of videos and wall-racks of shoes make it one of the most distinctive.

Until Olympus, there were fears that Sears would find it difficult to shake off the shadow of its former master, the late Sir Charles Clore. He was a financier and property magnate, rather than a retailer, and because of that background he was one of the first to spot how undervalued shop properties had become after the Second World War. He did not buy indiscriminately, but voraciously, and found shoe shops the easiest to amass.

When he took over J. Sears, as it then was, for £4 million in 1953 it already owned 500 Freeman Hardy Willis shops and 200 Trueform. There were rich pickings to be had from selling the freeholds on the shops and immediately leasing them back, but Clore realised that if he could compile a really huge shoe shop portfolio he would also acquire enough buying power to squeeze better deals out of the other manufacturers. So the next year he bought Curtess, two years later Manfield and Dolcis and in 1962 added Saxone and Lilley & Skinner.

As the list grew, so did his bargaining power. And the British manufacturers were weakened by the rising competition from Italy and the Far East. Clore was able to insist on exclusive ranges of shoes made to Sears' specification at special prices.

Clore bequeathed Sears a magnificent high street platform upon which to build. In recent years the group has added the names of Roland Cartier and Birthday Shoes and is testing the out-of-town shopping habit with Shoe City. They and the other shops in the group between them sell nearly one in every four shoes worn in Britain. The next biggest footwear seller, Marks & Spencer, is about a quarter the size.

And Clore did not stop there. He secured his lines of supply by taking over factories that together turned Sears' British Shoe Corporation into the biggest shoemaker in the land at that time. It is an unavoidable labour-intensive process, so the bulk of the manufacturing work has gradually been absorbed by low-wage countries. But BSC makes about fourteen per cent of the shoes that find their way on to Sears' shelves, and they are generally the standard, bread-and-butter men's black shoes that will sell in good times and bad. Outside suppliers have had to take the strain of ups and downs in demand for more fashion-led styles.

To that powerful base, Clore added glamour and glitter. He stepped outside the shoe trade for the first time in 1959, when he bought Garrard and Mappin & Webb. Six years later he moved into department stores, which are also important shoe sellers. After a bitter takeover battle he acquired Lewis's Investment Trust, which had a chain of provincial stores. It also owned a retail jewel almost beyond price: Selfridges, second only to Harrods in the pantheon of great department stores.

That virtually completed Sears' expansion phase under Clore, although the William Hill bookmaking chain was added in 1970 to give a ready source of cash flow.

Clore died in 1979, but his influence has lived on through his solicitor and long-standing associate, Leonard Sainer, who succeeded Clore as chairman until 1985 and then became life president of the company. Sears is now run principally by Geoffrey Maitland Smith and Michael Pickard. Maitland Smith is an accountant recruited by Clore in 1971, becoming chief executive the year before Clore's death. Pickard, Maitland Smith's deputy, joined the group in September 1986 after his previous company, the brewer and tobacconist Imperial Group, was taken over by Hanson Trust.

However, the new team has yet to stamp its own distinctive mark on Sears. For several years the retail revolution appeared to pass by the group, and it was accused of lacking flair. The outside world is only gradually beginning to perceive precisely where Maitland Smith and Pickard are taking the group.

'Shoes are seen as high fashion nowadays,' said Pickard. 'Selling, ambience and colour co-ordination are all vital parts of the selling process. Dolcis and Roland Cartier, our two upmarket chains, need prime sites in the city centre shopping areas. There is intense competition for locations, because you've got to have the right shop for the right street.'

One of the common criticisms thrown up by market research is that many people cannot tell one shoe shop from another, and often cannot remember where they bought a particular pair. They go out to buy shoes, stop at a window display, and if they see a pair they like at a price they are prepared to pay, they go in. Brand loyalty has been minimal.

It is a problem that Sears is beginning to tackle. Pickard explained: 'We are taking firm action to acquire closer profiles and price separation, so that people become aware that they can get a different class of shoe from Roland Cartier than they will obtain at Saxone or Curtess, say, while Dolcis is aiming much more clearly at women's fashion shoes. We have reoriented the business to run it as a series of family operations and volume brands, and we are relying on the window displays to get the various messages across.'

Shoes are becoming more glamorous as they draw nearer to the fashion trade, but it is hard to persuade most people to buy more of them. The real headache for the trade has been the sneaker or trainer – the all-purpose casual canvas shoe that more and more people are wearing all week long, in every social and working situation.

Sears has captured its share of the trainer traffic through Olympus and other parts of the group, but meanwhile it has also been unobtrusively converting a large number of its shoe shops into other brand names selling clothes – like Adams, which has quietly become the second biggest children's wear chain after Mothercare. Nevertheless all of them, with the obvious exceptions of the jewellers Garrard and Mappin & Webb, still sell shoes.

Like other retailers, Sears has fallen in with the current concept of packaging a complete look. People are more inclined to buy shoes to complete a newly-selected outfit than to make a separate, special journey for them. Turning the idea on its head, Sears has taken concessions in other stores, particularly department stores, to put a shoe shop alongside a clothing department.

The group plays its portfolio of high street names like instruments in an orchestra, emphasising this one then that, softening another and introducing new names and ideas as gaps arise in the market. The current thrust, demonstated by the recent takeovers of Fosters menswear and Wallis fashions, is to reduce the group's dependence on shoes. This is likely to be confirmed by further takeovers in the clothing area.

Said Pickard: 'We are refocusing our activities, utilising our property portfolio to match changes in the market place. We have integrated distribution and computer systems, which makes it easier to switch managers, and we want to make the maximum use of our bulk-buying power.' As the group's British shops have combined sales of more than £1,000 million a year, that power is considerable.

All the shops have to earn their own keep, and are judged on profits struck after deducting up-to-date rentals for internal accounting purposes, whatever rent is actually being paid on them. The managers of each chain have to compete with one another for newly acquired or vacated sites.

'The user companies, as we call them, meet the property investment company and make bids for properties in terms of the rent they are willing to pay head office,' said Pickard. 'Occasionally you get two offering the same amount, in which case you just have to arbitrate in terms of the overall strategy, for instance we might be under-represented in one chain or we might want to give less emphasis to another chain. And we have to allow for the optimists and the pessimists among the divisional executives, the ones who tend to overbid and those who tend to be too cautious, just as in any other business.'

Sears is starting new chains all the time, as the market changes and head office discovers that the group is not covering a particular niche. Milletts is best known for duffel coats and wellington boots, so they have started Tracker for the walking market. Jargon is a spinoff from Fosters when that business was brought into the group.

'You grow one market out of another,' Pickard explained. 'The more strongly you identify a market with a particular brand, the more likely you are to leave gaps on either side of it. We are building on areas of expertise – still sticking to the same knitting, if you like, but using new wools. Specialist names work both for and against. You are more clearly defined, but you lose customers who perceive themselves as being outside that definition. The important thing is to have a customer-feel and be out and about a great deal to see what's going on, observing with your own eyes. The offering – the type of shop and the range of goods in it – and the location are the two most crucial factors.'

Those are qualities that Selfridges has in abundance. Indeed it has been one of the main reasons that Oxford Street to the west of Oxford Circus has gradually overshadowed the other half of the street, lying to the east of the circus. The rents are higher as more and more shops and other department stores have congregated as close as they can get to Selfridges, whose imposing building has dominated the district ever since it was opened by the American, Gordon Selfridge, in 1909.

One of Sears' early decisions after taking over the store in 1965 was to use the name to develop a chain of young fashion shops as Miss Selfridge. The first appeared in 1966 in part of the main store, but another 62 have been opened and there are plans to double that number.

It was an ingenious way of getting more mileage out of the Selfridge name for, as Harrods has discovered, it is very difficult to open duplicate branches of the department store round the country. They are simply different markets. In the London catchment area there is the spending power, and the constant flow of tourists, to support department stores on the grand scale. The building can be kept in the best condition, both inside and out, and the store can afford to stock the widest range of goods.

The provincial stores are more down-to-earth, selling more basic goods. On the other hand, out of London the department store blueprint has become the anchor point for the new shopping centres. They provide the basic reason for going there, even though once they have made the journey shoppers will inevitably visit the competing outlets nearby.

One type of retailing missing from the Sears portfolio is mail order, although it is no secret that Maitland Smith has tried to fill this particular gap. It would be a marvellous way for Sears to promote its brands and expand its buying power. In 1983 he had his eye on Empire Stores and Grattan, which he described as 'a very good toehold to get into the mail order business'.

That was in the wake of the decision by the Monopolies and Mergers Commission to prevent Great Universal Stores from taking over Empire, and ordering GUS to reduce its holding of Empire shares. Maitland Smith had talks with the directors of Empire and Gratton, of which Pickard used to be chairman. The price, however, stayed out of reach, although that may not always be the case.

SIR PHIL TOYS WITH THE COMPETITION

'People say the high street is dead,' said Sir Philip Harris, 'but there are a lot of people who still don't own cars, particularly the

Tesco in its Green Shield Stamps days, and in the style of an
American superstore.

Two of Sears' established high street shopfronts.

young, and there are a lot of traditional people, who just prefer to shop in the high street.' So Sir Phil's Harris Queensway group is hedging its bets by keeping one foot in his old stamping ground and putting the other foot out of town. Times Furnishing, Harris Carpets, Mad Max, Vogue Carpets, Vogue Living and Electric Supreme are in the streets, while Queensway, Carpetland, Ross and General George Carpets, Ultimate, Poundstretcher and Accent Home Style inhabit the wide open spaces.

Retailing is all one to Harris, who at 45 is personally worth around £100 million and does not mind too much where he sells or what he sells, so long as it is not high fashion. 'You can lose all your money on fashion,' he warned. 'Apart from that, if I thought the opportunity was right I could retail anything.' But having made his fortune in carpets and furniture he splashed out £30 million in 1986 on what many, including some of his co-directors, saw as an extravagant indulgence: Hamleys. In doing so he outbid some strong international competition including Woolworth, Britain's biggest toy retailer.

It did indeed seem a steep price for four toy shops, none of them freehold, and net assets of only £5 million. So Harris was paying £25 million for the goodwill and the name. But those who knew Sir Phil realised that there had to be more to it than that. Hamleys was extended to more than a dozen shops by the end of 1986. Harris said: 'This will be the prestige store in the Harris Queensway group. By 1988 it should be making profits of £10 million a year.' A payback of that speed makes the £30 million price look cheap.

What Harris saw, perhaps more clearly than his rivals, was how deeply Hamleys' unique name had been underexploited, first by the Lines family and then by Debenhams. The Regent Street flagship store had become to the toy world what Foyle's, in London's Charing Cross Road, is to the book world: everything seemed jumbled up. When the computer games boom took off, former Hamleys management boldly threw over most of the basement to the new craze. But there was no pressure to buy. So the kids simply queued up to play. It was the best free entertainment in town, as children are all too quick to spot. The place was packed – and the tills were idle.

That mistake was corrected before Harris came on to the scene, and he is spending £750,000 on brightening it up and tightening the management controls. 'The store was a mess,' said Sir Phil. 'We have tried to get some discipline into the people and some atmosphere into the store. And we're going to have someone out in Regent Street with a Hamleys umbrella to bring people in from their limousines: you'd be surprised how many of those we get here. But there hasn't been a store manager until now, and the suppliers were paid weekly instead of monthly. The bills just piled up. Only one man was allowed to sign orders, so if he wasn't around nothing got ordered. Putting it right is a question of good housekeeping and motivating the staff.'

Another move is to sell toys under Hamleys' own brand name. That will be an important defence against what is likely to be Hamleys' most dangerous competitor – Toys R Us, recently arrived from the US. Their approach is almost the opposite to Hamleys, using large sheds on the edge of town, but trying to offer the whole range of any particular toy. The only way Harris can block that is to develop a range of toys exclusive to Hamleys. 'Toys R Us is a super company,' said Sir Phil, 'but the stores are so cold. They have got no atmosphere. It's quite a different attitude. I won't go out of town with Hamleys for some time.'

Harris is one of retailing's toughest negotiators, a ranking confirmed by his welcome on to the board of Great Universal Stores, the mail order and retail group moulded in its modern form by the legendary Glaswegian, Sir Isaac Wolfson. A few months before the Hamleys deal GUS took a 23 per cent stake in Harris Queensway in return for selling HQ the businesses of 341 Times Furnishing stores and 175 Home Charm do-it-yourself shops. GUS, canny as ever, kept the freeholds and long leases.

That tie-up was seen as the Wolfsons' way of signalling Sir Phil's status as heir apparent. The stock market promptly jumped to the conclusion that in the fullness of time GUS and Harris Queensway would merge so that Sir Phil could become overlord of the combined group and thereby one of the most powerful retailers in Britain. But much depends on how the two sides get on. No one is making commitments or promises until they have got to know one another better.

What GUS does have, along with the prestige store names of Burberrys and The Scotch House, is a dominant position in the mail order trade and a most sophisticated credit-rating system containing two million names and addresses. Harris Queensway is ready to learn from that system, as it is developing its own credit card, Impact, which is expected to have a million account holders by the end of 1987. That will make it the third biggest card in the country, after Barclaycard and Access. Each division of HQ – furniture, carpets, electrical, household and textiles and Hamleys – will have its own Impact catalogue and, significantly, the card is accepted in GUS outlets.

It is not Harris's first alliance with another leading high street name. In 1984 Debenhams struck a bargain under which Harris Queensway would buy sixty-five per cent of the shares in a new company to run furniture, electrical and carpet departments in Debenhams stores under the names of Vogue Living, Electric Supreme and Vogue Carpets. After Burton Group took over Debenhams the following year Harris bought the other thirty-five per cent stake in the operation and ran it as a concession.

It is a long way from the three modest carpet and linoleum shops in south London which Sir Phil's father owned, and where he himself started at the age of fifteen. Their first leap came in 1974, when they bought eighteen carpet shops trading under the name Keith Royle. Three years later Harris had a chain 93 strong, and that was when it went out of town by taking over Queensway Discount Warehouses operating thirty cut-price furniture and carpet 'sheds'. After a string of takeovers in the intervening decade, the group now runs more than 1,300 outlets, a remarkable rate of expansion that shows little sign of letting up.

Sir Phil has always been at his most comfortable selling to the suburban middle and working classes, and still shies away from challenging the top end of the carpet and furniture trade. 'That's really concentrated in the department stores, and you can't compete with the likes of John Lewis, there just isn't enough profit margin in it,' he conceded. His business succeeds by keeping things simple, holding costs down, computerising information and motivating staff to sell and give good service.

'The future of furniture lies in the design of the store,' he explained, 'because the product will not change much, compared to electricals. So we have to inject excitement into it. You've got to think how to make it exciting. You've got to get customers to touch, to get involved, then they get tempted. That's why we want more demonstrations at Hamleys. You've got to show them all the bits and pieces.'

That has been the aim behind the redesign of the Queensway chain. The new style is an integrated look, all in room settings, quite unlike the previously more spartan appearance. The difference costs £100,000 per store.

Logic nowadays points to encouraging shoppers to buy a whole kitchen at one go, not the individual items. The idea has been picked up from the fashion industry, which some years ago abandoned having different departments for skirts and blouses and knitwear. They tumbled that selling one garment doesn't make you as much money as selling three. And the colours never matched properly: the colour for that season might be green, but each buyer would buy a different shade of green.

Harris is applying the same thinking to furniture, by giving it more of a fashion element. Kettles, pots and pans always used to be in aluminium with black handles. Now they come in all sorts of colours and shapes and sizes. Fashion has come into the kitchen. But until recently if you bought a bed you probably went out of town, but you had to go back into town to buy the duvet, the sheets and the pillowcases. 'It was mad,' exclaimed Peter Carr, who was recruited from Debenhams to be managing director of Queensway. 'It's as if we said to them, thanks for buying the bed, now go away and get the rest elsewhere. We have to sell them the lot. So we are becoming more like a department store.'

To make that policy work, the salesperson has to learn about colour matching, and learn the skills of selling an associated product. The commission structures have been adjusted to reflect that, stepping it so the staff get maybe a half per cent for selling the suite then up to one per cent for the carpet, rather than the other way around.

The best way to get the public in a buying mood is to provide competition and choice. But the ironic price of Harris Carpets' success in the high street has been that the competition has wilted. So he invented his own brash, aggressive rival in the shape of Mad Max, which uses garish colours to pull the punters in and low prices to make them buy. Most of its stock sells for between £2 and £4 a square yard, compared with Harris Carpets' average of £7.50. 'You either love Mad Max or loathe it,' Harris grinned, carefully giving no clue about his own feelings. He does not carry much stock in those shops, preferring to concentrate on showing the range then delivering from warehouses and fitting.

The biggest change in shopping in the past decade has been the reduction in the number of trips, because more women work and more families have cars. That has cut the proportion of impulse shopping for the bulkier and more expensive items, and placed more of an onus on the retailer to clinch a sale there and then, because the chance may be lost for good.

The pressure has been intensified by Britain's demographic shift. The population is static, and the vital fifteen to twenty-four age group – source of first-time home and furniture buyers – is shrinking. Families are getting smaller. But more money is being spent on the home as house ownership has increased. And the previous generation of owner occupiers is dying, leaving substantial sums to their offspring.

Meanwhile better living standards and more central heating have opened up opportunities for selling softer, thinner materials, like leather or plastic, and brighter colours. That has in turn placed a higher premium on design.

'The customer has become more selective, more demanding, and price has become less important,' said Harris. What has grown more important is the availability of convenient and sophisticated credit facilities, and the indications are that this will be a major thrust of Harris Queensway's business in the next few years, with more than a little help from Great Universal Stores.

KALMS AT THE EYE OF THE STORM

'We sell toys for adults' is how Stanley Kalms disarmingly explains the philosophy behind Dixons, the aggressively successful retailer of televisions, radios, hi-fi, telephones, computers and so much else of the electronic gadgetry we love to clutter our homes with.

Kalms, Dixons' chairman, started in the camera trade. His father had been a portrait photographer in Edgware, north

London, but as cameras became cheaper and easier to use the demand for studio portraits lessened. young Stanley, then in his teens, decided to sell the hardware instead. 'I think I was always an entrepreneur,' he said. 'I was always trading in something, ever since I was twelve or thirteen.' Now he reckons to put his goods in every room in the house, from the phone in the hallway to the microwave oven in the kitchen, not forgetting the second television that perches on the end of the bed.

The company has since expanded beyond the scope of a one-man band. There is a certain arrogance about the people who run Dixons today, but it is the arrogance of men who know they are good at what they do. Alongside Kalms is the deputy chairman, Egon von Greyerz, who runs the money side of things, and Mark Souhami in charge of buying. They are the ruling triumvirate. To the Dixons chain they have added Currys for white goods like washing machines and refrigerators, and Kalms retains his old links with the photographic trade not only through Dixons but also by owning the upmarket Wallace Heaton series of camera shops.

The top managment's collective arrogance shone through in Dixons' attempt to take over Woolworth Holdings in 1986, a bid that was finally thwarted by a determined defence on the part of Woolies and the loyalty of the Prudential and a few other big shareholders. Kalms unashamedly campaigned on the platform that his team could run Woolies better than the existing manage-ment, describing the variety chain as 'a shambles'. Only by the skin of their teeth did Woolworth plead successfully for more time to get their act together.

Souhami has said that he sees the growth of Dixons Group coming from increasing the number of retail operations that they run. But Kalms is more cautious, possibly because of his one notable failure, the takeover and subsequent sale of Westons the chemists in the late 1970s. 'I don't think we need any more fascias,' he said. 'There is no overlap among the ones we have, and each has a sufficient customer base. Dixons is for men, Currys for women. I think we have got it perfect.'

He is dismissive of most of his fellow shopkeepers. 'Retailing is now the hotspot focus of the economy,' Kalms claimed, 'but there are still a lot of deadbeats in the high street. They are there for historical reasons and most will be taken over. People like Boots are living in yesterday's world. All they have are historically good sites. It's not enough to be in the high street if all you can offer is convenience. The high street is aggressive. It's about being product-led. Too many retailers are not product-led. They have existed on low sales and high margins, but there is no room for that now. You've got to be tough, young, dynamic, professional, with a story to tell. Body Shop is a supreme nothing, but it's got a story and unique products so it adds up to a great something. It's all come about because the economy went flat with heavy goods manufacturing, and more and more skills went into retailing, No other country has such a concentration of retailing talent.'

Kalms is a great believer in the idea of retailing as a precision engineering industry. In his view the stores need minute attention to detail and fine adjustments all the time. Lines of vision have to be right. Signs and price tickets must be clear and correctly positioned. Light, heat and noise levels must be set at just the right levels. The shops must be packed with goods to create excitement, making full use of the space.

'If you want space, go for a walk in the park,' Kalms declared. 'Your shops have to say "come in". The customer likes to wander round and touch. I can see what makes people move around a shop, what they want to see. I can see things that are wrong. It may be a speck of dust, a ticket out of place, a showcard placed too low, a warm spot under the lights, a fifteen-second delay at the counter, any of these things. It's about creating as perfect an environment and structure as you can. Nothing should be random. It should be as orderly as you can get. You have to get people in off the street, give them absolute and total confidence, and motivate them upwards so they will buy to the maximum they are comfortable with.'

To get customers in the mood for spending more than they originally intended, the emphasis is on making them feel relaxed, not under pressure. Dixons trains its salesmen to make contact very informally at first, to get away from the 'Can I help you' cliche and just say 'I'm here if you need me'. 'We do tend to be more formal, more restrained, in this country than in America,' said Kalms, 'but I believe we have a higher degree of integrity. "Have a nice day" is just so much bullshit.'

The sales pressure may be exerted when the customer is trying to decide which of two identical brands to buy, but the staff would reckon to have established a relationship by then. 'When you are dealing with durable goods there is no doubt that there is a greater degree of urgency,' Souhami admitted, 'because if you don't hit them that time round you haven't got them back again next Tuesday.'

However, before a shop can get the goods moving off the shelves, it has to make sure that it has the right goods on the shelves in the first place. Dixons regards its buying skills as the entrepreneurial guts of the business. The buyers are given incentives to take risks and correct them quickly if they make a mistake. They have got to know which products have done well or badly in the US or Japan or Europe, and when they have made a choice they have to pick the right price and know which features of the product to play up. 'Our whole concept is to keep on adding to the ranges,' Kalms explained. 'In all products you have natural additions. I've been trying to nag Currys into selling cookery books. Mind you, we give them away as a promotion with cookers and so on.'

As standards of living have risen, so more of Dixons' stock has become regarded by consumers as essential rather than luxury. Who could survive without a colour television nowadays? Consequently the electrical goods industry has become more fundamental to the market place. That has given Dixons the opportunity to put themselves across as the company of record, the yardstick supplier in the areas in which it operates. 'The fact that many of these markets are all found under one roof is a bonus,' said Souhami, 'but you push each market individually to the people who are in that market at that time, whether it is videos or telephones.'

Dixons keeps an open mind about the rival attractions of the traditional high street location and the out of town site. Its outlets are in some of the shopping centres, but Kalms is sceptical of the rush to the outskirts. 'High street and out of town are one market, not two,' he said. 'Most people use both, when it suits them. I do not think that out of town is a total proven success beyond certain industries. It is right for big furniture, which needs big space. There has to be a reason for going out of town, and that can only be the need for space. So the question remains unresolved. I do not think out of town is a gold mine. It's a silver mine, it's worth digging for. As a complement to furniture, there is a good case for us being there with televisions. That's fine. But there is no reason for going out of town to buy a camera.'

Kalms can afford to take a relaxed view about how far he needs to chase customers. Electrical goods have been an exciting business to be in, because the effective price of many of the products has fallen dramatically while the improvements in them have been equally spectacular. A television is thirty per cent cheaper than it was a few years ago, it has far more features and costs far fewer hours' work to pay for it. In 'real' terms, after allowing for inflation, it is about a quarter of the price it was.

'Our business is a vast replacement business,' said Kalms. 'Everyone has got a camera, a TV, a radio, whatever. So we have got to say this is better than what you have got. So it's about bringing replacement down to a shorter time cycle, getting people to renew more often. In the US it's even faster than here. People buy a radio for 15 dollars to take to the ball game half a dozen times, and they don't expect it to last longer than that. In England, someone will buy a radio for £10 and bring it back three years later complaining that it has gone wrong. You have got to explain that cheaper products have a shorter life cycle.'

Nevertheless, Kalms admits that 99 per cent of the goods he sells develop a fault during their life. So Dixons has an enormous service operation to turn repairs round rapidly. The life cycles of the gadgets are in any case continually being shortened by the speed at which improvements are introduced. Much of what Dixons sell is already obsolete, because they know that what will be coming on to the market next year will be even better. Whenever they think that a product has reached the final state of the art and cannot possibly be improved, a better version lands on their desk. This is of course manna from heaven for a retailer, because it means that he has always got a new story to tell the public, something to shout about.

To ensure that their stories are as new as anybody else's, Dixons have joined the growing trend for shopkeepers to develop close relationships with suppliers.

'We are normally in at the beginning of a new product,' said Kalms. 'They don't just come to us with a finished product and say "What do you think?" We go to Japan and see what's happening in two or three years' time. The good manufacturer will discuss with us the features and the price points. Or we will design it and take it to a manufacturer. We will invest in it and divide the cost of the tools with the manufacturer. With us it's a very interesting relationship. It's sound, solid, but not too comfortable. I do not believe in having comfortable relationships with everybody. You have to keep your commitments, but you don't have to renew your commitments. Some manufacturers used to like supplying small retailers because they could kick them around, but manufacturers try to work with retailers like us rather than fight us. You have to recognise that the manufacturer has to be able to start his production line on a Monday morning, and they have to provide a competitive edge to get on our shelves. So you are mentally trying to reserve space, deciding what to phase out in two years' time.'

Kalms is a firm believer in letting the customer touch the goods. 'The best way of selling is to let them touch and play with the merchandise,' he said. 'If you can get it into the customers' hands you have done almost everything you want to do. The essence of selling is touching.' But allowing people to touch has one drawback: it encourages theft.

That puts Dixons and others in a dilemma. The more touchable the goods are, the more they sell but the more people steal. Kalms argues that the interface between touchability and shrinkage, as theft is euphemistically known in the trade, could become a major issue in retailing. The trouble is that security technology is running slightly behind the shrinkage rate. As shops become more open and attractive they become more tempting to those who cannot enjoy touching without stealing. And it can happen in any area. It is not particularly a feature of the areas which have been scarred by riots. It tends to occur more frequently in areas which have hitherto been seen as affluent and calm, but are suffering from the currently inevitable percentage who are unemployed and unoccupied.

'Society will have to become more and more protective as we find the haves and have-nots eyeballing each other,' Kalms predicted. 'It's a social tragedy. One doesn't want to pit modern technology against people. It's an unfair battle. You don't want to catch people, you want to prevent theft happening.'

One non-threatening way of keeping an eye on the stocks is through the use of electronic point-of-sale terminals, or EPOS. These record the details of every sale and pass them back to a central computer. So for the first time the retailer can see what is selling and what isn't, what his stock position is and how much profit he is making on each item. And it gives him an abundance of statistics and data, so he can compare through time what the trends are. Kalms explained: 'The secret of retailing is to panic quickly. When you go in on a Monday morning you need to know what's been moving and what hasn't, what you've got too much of and what you're short of. Then you can react accordingly.'

Dixons is a company which is beginning to flex its muscles. It has assembled the management, systems, administration, funds, a high level of profit and a good return for its shareholders. The question now is whether it can make that leap from the middle reaches of the first division to the top as the retailer on every other retailer's lips. The bid for Woolworth was an attempt to make that leap. 'We learnt a lot from that,' said Kalms. 'They put up a good defence, but there were three big institutions against us who felt they had to stick with Woolworths. After all, we were only trying to buy something. If someone doesn't want to sell, what can you do? We simply asked the question.'

It is a question that is likely to be asked by Dixons several times more in the future. The management is ready for new challenges, and Kalms clearly wants to make his mark on the high street.

The Golden Oldies

THE PROTAGONISTS:
- *W H SMITH*
- *BOOTS THE CHEMIST*
- *WOOLWORTHS*

In the battle for the high street, it is all too easy to overlook the Golden Oldies – those chains that seem to have always been around, but must now adapt or perish in the highly competitive world that retailing has now become.

When Boots and W H Smith opened their first shops, around the turn of the century, they were themselves doing something quite new. They were relying on their fame and reputation spreading by word of mouth, so that whenever anyone saw a branch of Boots or Smith's, they would know what range of goods it stocked, and what price and standard they would be sold at. They were reliable.

Reliability was an important asset at a time when the high street was full of one-off shops, which had to build their reputation painstakingly. The multiples, as they came to be known, could reinforce their reliability by buying in bulk direct from the best manufacturers, and arguing for the best prices into the bargain. Then they could shout about their advantage by advertising on a scale that their smaller rivals could not contemplate.

The fiercest retail competition a hundred years ago, as today, was in food, because that was all most people could afford to buy on a regular basis. But as standards of living rose the high street's range widened, from clothes and furniture to books and newspapers, and electrical goods.

Until recently, the battle in the high street has been largely an economic one, about getting prices down and lines of distribution improved. The multiples had enough to concentrate on with the business of opening enough branches and pushing the independent shopkeeper to one side.

The new factor has been the challenge to the supremacy of the long-established multiples. They still dominate the high street, to the extent that no property developer can hope to get good retail rents without first attracting some of the big names. But newcomers are nibbling away at that supremacy, whether it is drugstores snapping at Boots' heels or record shops and newsagents attacking Smith's.

In some cases the fresh competition is offering a better service than the established names can provide, because they are more flexible or give their staff better incentives. The most straightforward way to compete has been by opening for longer hours to catch the emergency or impulse purchase.

But big chains are also vulnerable to a more serious and fundamental form of competition. Simply because they have always been there in the eyes of the present generation, they can be made to appear fuddy-duddy. They are the shops that mother and father always used to go to and swear by for those little necessities like a bag of sweets, a bottle of aspirin or a packet of envelopes. Therefore generations have grown up being taken to these 'golden oldies' of the retail world by their parents.

While it is all too natural to want to rebel against parental practices, until the 1960s and 1970s there were few realistic alternatives to the established chains. The independents were licking their wounds, and retailing was not an industry that many bright young talents gravitated towards. Besides, up to the end of the 1950s younger shoppers did not have enough spending power to make it worth while catering to their whims.

That has changed. And the impact of design has shown how it is possible to offer a new and different retail story to a particular market at little extra cost. What Quant could do in fashion and Conran in furniture, imitators could apply to other types of retailing.

At first, the likes of Woolworths, Boots and W H Smith did not react. The new breed of competition appeared to be making few noticeable inroads, and with hindsight the retailing establishment underestimated the profound influence design would have in creating excitement and making shopping less of a chore. They also underestimated the willingness of the new shopping public to try something new as a way of making their demands felt.

They have begun to react now. W H Smith has taken the most radical line. In taking over some of the fresh competition like Our Price, it has effectively decided to follow the consumer across the street, implicitly conceding that its core chain can no longer appeal to everyone. The others have tried to adapt, calling in the designers and widening or rearranging the mix of products they offer.

It is no coincidence that in the meantime they have been spotlighted by the stock market as potentially vulnerable to takeover bids, although the Smith family still has a strong shareholding with which to ward off predators. In 1986 Woolworth escaped by the skin of its teeth from being swallowed by the more aggressive Dixons Group, and it is still too early to say whether the new management can secure the independence of a chain that has become a relic of a bygone era.

It is hard to believe that a former manager of Woolworths could recall: 'We reckoned that a Woolworths manager was the highest-paid manager of any retail store in his town. We had some managers with Rolls-Royce motor cars. I could send my children to north Wales for six weeks in the summer with my chauffeur and my cook and nanny, and my wife and I could then go away on a fortnight's cruise.'

Though it has not recovered to quite that pre-war level, the affluence of the average store manager is beginning to grow again, as salaries are bid up in the more competitive environment. But it is no easier for an old retail chain to don a new and trendy garb than it is for an elderly person to dress like a punk. Every chain appeals to a certain audience, even if that audience may be shrinking. The danger of a facelift is that it can alienate what is left of the old audience before it has time to lure the intended new audience.

So the golden oldies are at a crossroads. Unless they can make the transition to the type of shopping environment that prevails today they will become left behind. Woolworths may already have left it too late. Although the others in this category are in nothing like as desperate a state, they can no longer afford to be complacent. Too much is changing, too quickly.

W H SMITH: FROM A PAPER ROUND TO DO IT ALL

W H Smith is part of the high street's fixtures and fittings. It seems as if it has always been there, to the extent that no high street feels complete without one of its shops. That is no mere illusion: it is borne out by commercial reality. Any property developer rebuilding a street, or planning a shopping centre, makes a bee-line for Smith's and one or two others like Boots and Marks & Spencer.

Once they have agreed to come in, other retailers queue to take space alongside them because of the numbers they attract. So the prophecy becomes self-fulfilling.

Smith's, despite its carefully-nurtured cosy image, has long been aware of its own worth. William Henry Smith, son of the original W H Smith, seized the opportunity of placing bookstalls on station platforms in the 1840s. But they pulled out smartly in 1906 when the railway managements tried to extract too much rent. Instead, Smith's built shops on the roads to the stations.

It all began in 1792, when Henry Walton Smith, the first W H's father, started a paper round in Mayfair. The first W H moved the business to the Strand, so that he was near Fleet Street and could wholesale papers round the country by stagecoach. Although the shops are now the biggest part of the business, wholesaling is still its backbone, providing the vital direct link with publishers.

The Victorian values of honesty and reliability have served the group well down the years. You have to trust a retailer who sells you a book or a record, or even a magazine, and people do not expect to be ripped off when they go into a branch of Smith's. In any case, reading matter tends to be sold at a fixed price, which has made it hard for anyone to undercut the market leader.

For a long time Smith's escaped the retail revolution. But design and innovation have made their inroads. Some rivals have cleverly exploited the flip side of Smith's reputation for reliability: that they were all right for uncles and aunts, but not entirely in touch with a younger generation whose spending power was becoming a major force in the marketing of consumer goods.

It was perhaps at its most vulnerable in selling records, which Smith's had started as a way of replacing the space formerly taken up by lending library departments. These finally went in 1961, crushed by the tide of paperbacks. Like books, records were then sold at a fixed price and Smith's carried a big enough stock to ensure that would-be customers would not have a wasted journey.

But you do not make money by selling records to the over-40s. It has become a young and rebellious market, as chains like Virgin and Our Price have demonstrated. For several years Smith's accepted the loss of sales: they could hardly adapt their style to match that sort of competition. It was only when they noticed people walking out of Smith's and transferring their newly-bought records to an Our Price bag that they realised how badly they were missing out. So they took over Our Price, running it as a separate operation.

Malcolm Field, Smith's managing director, explained: 'Our Price gets us to a section of the record-buying market that we would not otherwise reach: younger people who according to our research felt that W H Smith was too stuffy. Our Price appeals to the younger generation. They feel more relaxed there, they meet their friends, they feel the staff is more knowledgeable, that the range of records is better. Smith's and Our Price together give us a very big share of the record market.'

The historically significant change that has taken place at Smith's is that the management has decided it can no longer be all things to all men. Retailing has become too fragmented for that. So it is indulging in a little kidology by repackaging itself under different names that appeal to different sections of the market it is selling to.

'We have segmented the market,' said Field. 'Retailing today is all about targeting: who are you after, what do they want, how do we get them? It's also about product: its quality and how you present it. We know about books, records, stationery. We have segmented them by developing Sherratt & Hughes as a specialist bookshop chain, Our Price for records and Paperchase for station- ery. Paperchase is for those who want something a bit different. It's in the fashion business. People are moving more in that direction.'

It is a measure of the fragmentation that some hearts sank on learning that Smith's were taking over their favourite chain, fearing that it would be turned into part of the newsagent network. But that, nowadays would be self-defeating. When the group opened a branch of its specialist bookshop in Leicester it produced a turnover of £800,000 a year, without having any effect on the book sales of the Smith's outlet in the town.

The group's strategy is to get more geographical coverage. Smith's shops have 1.7 million sq ft of space, and they believe that saturation would be two million. They have 40 specialist book- shops which could expand to 100. The present 170 record shops could go to 300.

'Retailing has come alive in the past two years,' Field said. 'It used to be a dull business, frankly. But now it has changed. I used to go to America to see what the new ideas were, but now I don't think they have anything to teach us. It has partly been a matter of catching up, and there has been a lot of takeover activity too. People are seeing new opportunities, and of course the consumer market has been buoyant for a few years. You've got to be thinking ahead, constantly asking "What do they want of us?" It's so easy to get it wrong. Consumers are very fickle, and if something is not quite right they are very quick to go somewhere else.'

The central theme of the Smith's 360 high street shops is to focus on a group of products that cater for people's spare time and leisure: newspapers, stationery, books and magazines, records, travel. They admit that there is no real logic to the mix: it is just something that has evolved piecemeal. They have a wider range of stationery than Rymans, and sell more of it than they do, giving Smith's thirty per cent of that market. The chain is stronger in magazines than newspapers, so much so that it is vital for publishers to get a new magazine into Smith's. They are less strong in newspapers because the high street doesn't open until 9 am, while the confectionery, tobacco and newsagents shops – known in the trade as CTNs – open at five or six o'clock for house-to-house deliveries. It is an area that Smith's is happy to miss out on.

Field explained: 'We could buy a CTN chain, but we think that market is ex-growth. Sales of confectionery, tobacco and newspapers are all static. I think the only way they are going to generate more growth is by shading into convenience stores, offering longer opening hours and microwave ovens to cook your own snacks. We will not go into that.'

Unlike a supermarket chain, most of the goods Smith's sells change all the time. Apart from the newspapers and magazines, new records are constantly coming out, there are 60,000 books published every year, and a back list of 350,000. These tides and eddies have to be superimposed on changing seasons and the Christmas rush. It presents a mighty stock control problem, particularly as the normal £100 million-worth of stocks is turned over every six weeks or so.

'We have 60,000 lines in our big stores,' Field pointed out. 'Electronic point-of-sale terminals are helping us to make sure that the right goods are available. There's nothing more annoying if you're giving a dinner party than to buy red napkins and red place mats and then find there are no red candles. On the other hand, we cannot afford to stock an obscure book that sells only one copy every year. You don't get depth in our high street shops, but there is a wide range. The depth is in our specialist bookshops, but some people don't like going in them. They feel daunted by them as if they were a library. There's a very academic atmosphere. But they can go into a Smith's and browse and there's lots happening, there are kids in there and it's much more informal. It's segmentation again.'

One difficulty Smith's faces, partly because of the nature of the business it is in, is making itself sufficiently different from its competitors to keep giving shoppers a reason to buy from them rather than somewhere else. After all, a lot of its goods are exactly the same as you can get elsewhere. It does not matter whether someone goes into Smith's or another shop to buy a book: it will be the same book. So, following the example of Marks & Spencer and the supermarkets, Smith's has gone in for the own-brand tactic. They have their own brand of stationery, Quality Bond, which has quickly overtaken Basildon Bond, the best seller for years on end. Superdrug sells Basildon Bond cheaper than Smith's, but of course it can't stock Quality Bond.

Smith's has also started to develop own-brand books, usually on bland but perennially popular subjects like illustrated books on dogs or cats. They go to a publisher like Hamlyn and guarantee to buy maybe 50,000 copies, leaving the editorial entirely up to the publisher. It must be exclusive to W H Smith, and says so, but only in a discreet line on the cover. 'I suppose we could call them the *W H Smith Book of Cats* or whatever, but we are not very good at blowing our own trumpet,' Field admitted.

Such modesty has made Smith's cautious about jumping on the design bandwagon in an attempt to lure more customers. The WHS cube logo was introduced fifteen years ago to smarten its image, and the shops' appearance has been cleaned up. A major facelift began last autumn as research showed that people were once again regarding Smith's as worthy but dull, and were not sufficiently aware of the previous exercise in modernisation. Brighter, lighter colours have been replacing the earlier shades of brown.

'What does design get you as a business? It gets you people in saying it's fun, I like it, I feel relaxed,' Field explained. 'Look at Marks & Spencer's food: it's always mouth-watering because the packaging is so well designed. But you have got to be careful with shops selling books because people are so sensitive about that. And I think the design changes will come home to roost. You have to re-fit anyway every so often, whether you change the design or not because fittings wear out. We hope our new design will last eight years, but some of the chains are redesigning faster and faster, to keep up with one another. Are they going to get the extra volume to pay for it? It's a nasty charge on the profit-and-loss account. I come back to my point that product is what matters. Marks & Spencer was very drab for a long time. Lord Rayner, the new chairman, is now changing it, but not a lot. It's mainly cardboard engineering, if you look closely.'

Nevertheless, the spring-cleaning mood has caught the group strongly enough for them to embark on a redesign of their Do It All chain of out-of-town do-it-yourself stores. the DIY 'sheds', as they are known, are all beginning to look like one another, so Smith's is trying to steal a march by looking distinctively different and more entertaining.

Smith's went into DIY because it was amassing spare cash and needed a new retailing activity. More leisure time is being devoted to decorating the home rather than curling up with a magazine, so more leisure-time spending is being diverted to weekend family trips out of town. 'DIY is a £2 billion-a-year market,' said Field, 'and the key is getting prime sites. They used to be stand-alone, but now the thing is to combine into retail parks to pick up one another's traffic. Just as Smith's, Marks & Spencer and Boots used to constitute a high street, so now Currys, MFI and a Do It All make up a retail park. It adds up to a worthwhile shopping trip.

It also adds up to a worthwhile retailing opportunity, but Smith's soon found that they had to learn plenty in a short time. The trouble was that the sector was expanding so rapidly that there were not enough trained managers to keep up with the growth in the number of sheds. Those with the right experience have been happily moving from firm to firm, raising their salary with every turn of the merry-go-round. Do It All's managing director has been promoted from another division of Smith's but the next tier all come from the supermarket trade.

Do It All has concentrated on core DIY, taking a leaf out of Smith's high street strategy by offering an across-the-board service. They have made mistakes, and they are still learning, but the venture has been successful enough to prompt the question whether the W H Smith chain may reduce its commitment to the high street and have more of an out-of-town presence. It is already in some of the big shopping centres, which are effectively the high street by another name.

'I believe that the trend to the edge of town has been purely a matter of convenience,' said Field. 'You don't want to hump a bag of cement along the high street. But I don't think edge-of-town sites will replace the high street. They aren't busy during the day. It's mainly lunchtimes, evenings and weekends. The high street is entertainment, fun, and retailers have realised this. That's what the whole design thing is about. Chore shopping, such as food, will go out of town, but fashion won't. Everyone talks about Marks & Spencer quitting the high street, but they won't, and nor will we. We both have some out-of-town sites, like Brent Cross in north London or the Metro Centre near Gateshead, but they will be in addition to the high street locations.'

CHILD'S PLAY FOR BOOTS

Boots is one of a rare breed, a long-established company that has always defied the conventional wisdom that it is a mistake to try to combine retailing and manufacturing. While the group has had some notable successes in developing drugs, and in 1986 spent £400 million buying Flint Laboratories of the US, its shops have come under sharp competition from the new drugstores that are springing up round the country, from Share Drug and Superdrug to Tip Top and Underwoods. It is no longer enough to have a pharmacist in a white coat handing out prescriptions: the dazzle factor, which has swept through much of the rest of the high street, is beginning to shake up the chemist's shops.

Like W H Smith, Boots is a company whose strategy is determined by decisions made many years ago. The group's factories were originally conceived and built by Jesse Boot to provide merchandise to sell through the stores. That took the company naturally into the production of research-based pharmaceuticals.

Keith Ackroyd, the managing director of Boots' retail division, said: 'We are manufacturers as well as retailers, but we have to start from where we were. In a way, it would be nice not to have to bother with manufacturing, but we have it and that's that. We have been doing this for a century. If one was going to another planet, I am not saying this is the way to do it.' The internal tension pervading those remarks bears testimony to the constant competition for resources between the retail and industrial divisions.

Robert Gunn, the present chairman, has spent most of his career with Boots on the retail side. As director of shop development, he was responsible for doubling the group's retail space in the 1970s. But he was running the industrial division for the last few years before he became chairman. Now he has to decide priorities between the two, planning a foray into the out-of-town retail market on the one hand, and on the other buying Flint in the teeth of opposition from his shareholders, some of whom thought he was paying too much.

Gunn explained: 'We don't have a problem in allocating resources. We do it according to the propositions that come up from the divisions. We have an idea of the overall strategy, but we have money in the bank and if a good proposition comes up we can finance it any day of the week, provided it stands up and gives the right return on capital.'

The two divisions are run quite separately. The industrial division supplies competing retailers, making the Crooks range of products for example, and the retail side is reasonably free to stock its shelves with the output of other suppliers. 'We have arrangements between us about whether they are the preferred supplier,' said Ackroyd. 'It would be going it a bit for us to say they were having to compete for our business, but the arrangement can change from time to time.'

In some areas that arrangement suits both sides very nicely. Boots may not be the first name that springs to mind in cosmetics, yet it is the biggest manufacturer of cosmetics in the country, under the brands No 7 and No 17, which appear only in Boots shops. Together they account for about one seventh of the UK market.

The group's historical emphasis on pharmaceuticals has instilled the need for pharmaceutical quality control, and that has influenced quality control of other goods. More than a decade ago, Boots saw the need to apply similar standards to non-pharmaceuticals, particularly those marketed under Boots' brand name: garments, electrical goods, cameras. The specification may come from Boots or from the suppliers, and if necessary Boots will tell a supplier if he ought to be making a certain product. Or they have the option of making it themselves. Boots produces its own home wine-making and brewing kits, where again it is the biggest in the country.

Nearly everyone in Britain – 98 per cent, according to the company's own figures – goes to Boots. Half go every fortnight. That puts a different perspective on the retail targeting that the likes of Sir Ralph Halpern are so fond of. In a large proportion of the goods Boots offers, the customers' needs are identical, but if virtually the whole population is already visiting your shops, growth is going to be generated only by persuading everyone to buy more or buy better. Some areas, such as cosmetics, are ripe for a targeted approach. Women are buying better lipsticks and perfume than ten years ago and are going more up-market. The recent relaunches of No 7 and No 17 have been distinctly more sophisticated than the comparable exercises two launches ago.

'We are about getting each customer to trade up,' said Ackroyd. 'It's aspirational, though I'm not sure what that means. People have become more demanding of quality and service. That means better ambience, cleanliness, style and packaging. We have provided our customers more space and a wider range of merchandise, because that is what they tell us they want. We have our own brands and the width of a proprietary range. We have introduced more design to create the right sort of atmosphere in special sectors like Cookshops and Sound & Vision.'

Like Smith's, Boots has had to wrestle with its inheritance to keep it up to date with the changing needs and wants of the modern consumer, whilst retaining the best of its enduring standards. A typical Boots branch in 1950 sold a range of merchandise which would be broadly recognisable today: pharmaceuticals, toiletries, baby products, kitchen gadgets, giftware, stationery. It was no coincidence that Jesse Boot's wife was the daughter of a Jersey stationer.

But in those days Boots also had a picture department, selling pictures and mirrors. And it was famous for its lending library, where every book was emblazoned with a Boots sticker. Like Smith's, it had to abandon the library in the face of competition from cheap paperbacks. It used to sell radios, but for many years shied away from having a record department. Computers are of course a recent addition. Boots used to have cafés in its bigger shops, dropped the idea, but is going back into them in the form of coffee shops to create interest and to help draw customers into the upper floors, the perennial bugbear of any multi-level retailer. Boots has faced that problem more often as it has been opening bigger branches lately.

'We do offer variety and price, even if that is not fashionable any more,' said Ackroyd. 'If you think of the old Woolworths, their sales area was 10 million square feet and ours was half that. We expanded our sales area enormously in the 70s and our profits tailed off. We are now making our size work harder. We have spent a lot of time doing that. The old Woolworths never got away from its "Nothing over 6d" slogan in people's minds. I cannot remember many upper-class people wanting to go into Woolworths in those days, but they did and do come into Boots.'

But although Boots reckons that its level of traffic is as good as ever it was, the people who make up that traffic are not spending as readily as they once were. Sales recorded by the Boots the Chemist chain in the UK rose by only 5.5 per cent in the year to March 31, 1986, barely ahead of the rate of inflation. In terms of the number of goods being taken off the shelves, the position was static.

The fact is that more people are spreading their spending on Boots' range of goods more widely, from supermarkets to drug stores. Boots aims to draw people into its branches for the basic toiletries and drugs, and then tempt them to buy something else. But two can play at that game. The supermarkets are pushing the idea of one-stop, once a week shopping harder than ever, and have cottoned on to the idea of alluring and well-lit toiletries shelves. The drug stores are catching more of the passing trade. Boots has been forced to respond by being more price competitive.

The group has also had to streamline its management structure to ensure that it can react more swiftly to changes in the market. In what amounts to the biggest shake-up for sixty years, Boots has decreed one set of management for the 200 large stores of over 600 square metres, and one for the 800 others. The smaller stores have an area management layer and district managers each controlling about fifteen stores in a much more hands-on approach than before. In the big stores the branch managers are left with more individual responsibility. 'We realised that the smaller shops are in need of a different type of control,' said Ackroyd.

Cutting across that set-up are nine business areas, one for each product group such as chemist's, perfume, baby products and so on. Each one has a manager in charge of marketing, pricing, negotiation, merchandising.

Ackroyd explained: 'We have introduced that to get accountability into the organisation. It had become difficult to see who was accountable for what. Many people had an input, but it was difficult to see who was actually responsible for implementing a decision once it had been made. Before, we have marketed a store, and it has been a compromise. Now the Sound & Vision manager will see Dixons as his competitor, while the Perfumes manager will be looking at a different set of competition. We want to get some of that thrust decentralised. So we are having general managers for each business. But it is not as chaotic as it sounds: design and advertising, the stores themselves and responsibility for the products will be separate. And there is provision for settling disputes between the managers of two business areas.'

The scheme has haunting echoes of the now-discredited system installed by the former directors of Debenhams, before the department store group was taken over by Burton in 1985. That turned out to be a formula for internecine warfare. Naturally, Boots is confident that it will not fall into the same trap. A more radical solution would be for Boots to let each product group have its own chain of shops. Other chains have tinkered with this and after Boots took over Timothy White and Taylor in 1968 it turned some of those branches into houseware shops, but they were soon amalgamated with the rest of the group.

'We found that the sales intensity of that merchandise was increased when we brought them under the same roof,' said Ackroyd. 'The only reason I can think of for it working better that way is that you would have to open a Timothy White's door to buy a piece of their houseware, but you might be in Boots already buying something else.' Optical departments have been introduced since the recent change in the law, and as if in vindication of the shop-within-shop strategy they were immediately giving above-average numbers of eye tests compared with the established opticians.

That is why the main Boots chain is committed to the high street. It relies on customer traffic, people popping in to buy a bar of soap because they happen to be passing, and then stopping to buy something else that catches their eye. Or, just as valuable, the emergency shopper who will go to Boots because it is round the corner or just down the road. For those reasons it is less exposed to comparison shopping, though people do inevitably compare over a series of visits. Underwoods, Share Drug and Top Drug scream out at the passing trade, as if to say 'Come in and try us!' And that is precisely what they want the passer-by to do. Many consumers travel on automatic pilot for those routine purchases like a tube of toothpaste or a bottle of shampoo. The task of the newcomers to the chemists' business is to alter those automatic pathways in their own favour.

Lower prices help, as Boots has been forced to recognise, at least in the toiletries area where competition is fiercest. It has fought back by advertising on the slogan that You Can't Buy Cheaper. The group has also abandoned the policy of universal pricing throughout the chain, instead letting local managers take on nearby price-cutters. This has given Boots much-needed flexibility in what is a much more fluid market than hitherto.

'High streets are going to continue,' said Ackroyd. 'Planning constraints will prevent the high street dying, but there is no doubt that some of the secondary and tertiary streets are at risk. There can be no standard Boots format for a town of 50,000 or more. People in Birmingham expect to have a big Boots on several floors, while elsewhere they will be used to a small branch. We would be reluctant to build on a greenfield site. But we are in the Metro Centre and Brent Cross, which are high streets by other names. We have tried building across from a free-standing supermarket, but people want to get back in the car and get home once they get out of the supermarket.'

Nevertheless, Boots felt it was missing out on the public's growing acceptance of the out-of-town shopping habit. To get in on that act, it had to come up with a formula which would add up to enough of an event for people to make a special trip. The answer, which made its bow in 1987, was Childrens World with first stores in Dudley, Leicester and Cricklewood, north London. The need it is trying to meet is for a one-stop store that provides everything for children up to ten years old, the years when parents normally have to traipse them round from shop to shop, exhausting both adult and child in the process. The stores have been kitted out in bright red, blue and yellow, with wide aisles for pushchairs, the parents' equivalent of the supermarket trolley. Children can enter the store on a slide, and there is a glass-walled lift to the upper gallery.

On sale are clothes, shoes, books, toys, games, party goods, haircuts, nursery furniture and maternity wear. Feeding and changing rooms, together with a kids' restaurant and play areas, are there to cope with emergencies and keep the youngsters amused. So Childrens World is competing with Mothercare, Marks & Spencer, Adams, Benetton, W H Smith and McDonalds – quite a tall order on the face of it. Concessions have been sold to Dash and Benetton 012 clothes, Clarks and Start-rite shoes and Snips Hairdressing. The managing and marketing directors, Alan Ripley and Ron Glaister, are Boots men, but they have also recruited people from Littlewoods, BhS, Debenhams, Allders, Marks & Spencer and Asda.

Although Boots has been selling children's goods for several years through its Baby Boots departments, Childrens World represents a considerable departure for the group, involving some totally new skills.

'We wanted to get into the edge-of-town market,' said Gunn, 'and we went through a number of different policies before we came up with this one. We didn't want to compete with Harris Queensway and the DIY chains. We wanted something different that we could do professionally. We couldn't stick a Boots in a greenfield site, because people won't jump in a car just to get a tube of toothpaste. But Childrens World is one-stop shopping for everything parents need to buy for children.'

Boots is spending £100 million to compile a chain of between thirty and forty Childrens World stores round the country, each of about 30,000 sq ft. It is a gamble. If the idea does not catch on, its abandonment would leave morale in the retailing division at a low ebb and in poor shape to face the relentless high street battle to hold on to what used to be a comfortable and easily defended market share. The second alternative is more exciting but no less worrying. If Childrens World does well it will attract competition from other retailers with considerably more experience in that market.

Either way, while Boots' pharmaceutical side can look forward to launching some potentially money-spinning drugs in the next few years, the retailing division still has much to do to show it can cope with the new pressures – both more severe and more volatile – that are now engulfing the high street.

VARIETY IS THE SPICE OF LIFE

As Woolworth is proud to point out, there are only two retail groups in Britain that are as well known by their nicknames as by their proper titles – Woolies and Marks and Sparks. Every retailer likes to be bracketed in some way with M & S, possibly in the hope that some of the M & S magic will rub off on them. Few have had more cause to dream that dream than Woolworth, whose reputation had long since been buried when its American parent sold the British end of the business in 1982. It was a retailing story that had grown stale in the retelling, and at first there were few volunteers to help rekindle public enthusiasm. But Woolies is beginning to look its competitors in the eye without flinching.

Frank Winfield Woolworth had been running his American chain for thirty years when he opened his first British branch in Church Street, Liverpool on November 5, 1909 – coincidentally the same year that another American, Gordon Selfridge, unveiled his opulent emporium in London's Oxford Street. Woolworth had founded his operation on the simple idea of selling as many goods as possible for either five or ten cents apiece. He translated that to England with the same degree of variety, pricing items at a penny, threepence or sixpence. He also insisted on buying direct from manufacturers, another innovation. The 'nothing over sixpence' slogan became Woolworth's motto until the Second World War, although it lingered in the public mind for long after and latterly came to dog the group.

The Woolworth stores were a sensation. They were big and open, and encouraged people to stroll about without any direct pressure to buy. Frank Woolworth once recalled the standard British shop of those days: 'The moment you go in you are expected to buy, and to have made your choice from the window. They give you an icy stare if you follow the American custom of just going to look round.' On the first two trading days 60,000 people visited the pioneer Liverpool store. A second branch was opened in Preston, and then another in Liverpool, when the sales counters were pushed about the floor by the initial crush of shoppers, who helped themselves while assistants fainted.

After the 1914-18 war the chain expanded rapidly, opening a branch a week at one stage, until by 1931 it had 434 branches and the American parent floated 48 per cent of the British company's shares on the London stock market. By then it could afford to pay for its senior managers to celebrate in the ballroom of the Savoy Hotel in London.

Branch managers' pay was tied to the trading and profits of the store and made the managers of big branches wealthy men. Alexander Taft started as manager of the north London branch in 1928. He said: 'I did terribly well. I worked very hard. In two years they moved me to a bigger store, which was Richmond. I had that for a couple of years, increased the sales, increased the profits. I was rated as a pretty good operator so they gave me Kilburn. I was there for two years, I did the same thing. The great thing was to beat the average and be better than anyone else.'

Woolworth became a cornerstone of the high street. It could be relied on for the staple goods that everyone needs – food and clothing, haberdashery, hosiery, soft furnishings, lighting, paint – and had the buying power to bargain for keen prices, but not so keen that its suppliers did not also grow rich. The trouble was that the central idea got out of hand.

In the 1970s the group tried to go upmarket and out of town. It launched Woolco, the hypermarket chain which in many ways was years ahead of its time. But the notion of selling anything and everything was still writ on tablets of stone, and it got to the stage where no one in the company knew precisely how many lines they were stocking. Between 55,000 and 70,000 was the best estimate.

Stocks swelled to the point where they amounted to £500 million, equal to nearly half the yearly turnover. Two months' turnover would have been ample. As many as 9,000 lines sold fewer than five items per store per year, which indicated that stock control had got out of hand, and – even more ominous – that the group was losing touch with its customers.

In 1981 the then finance director wrote a confidential report to the board which said: 'It has been clear for a good many years that the UK Woolworth company has been on a downward profit slide compared to the profit performance of the competition and to its own past performance. The board and management have considered many options, but without a positive commitment. In consequence, with the passage of time, the company has become weakened and only reactive to incursions into its variety market. These reactions have usually been too late and ineffective.' It was to prove to be an epitaph.

Within a year a consortium of investment funds was put together to buy the American Woolworth's 52 per cent stake in the British operation and install a new management team led by John Beckett, former head of British Sugar, which had itself just been taken over. Beckett brought with him from his previous firm Geoff Mulcahy and Nigel Whittaker. None of them had any retail experience, and initially they had a hard time persuading high-flyers that joining Woolworth was a good career move. As the recovery has become evident they have senior executives from Asda, Sainsbury, House of Fraser, Littlewoods, W H Smith, Marks & Spencer and even Dixons, the electrical shops group which so nearly took over Woolworth after an epic struggle in 1986.

That struggle hinged on whether the present management, now headed by the ex-Unilever chairman, Sir Kenneth Durham, could complete the job of releasing Woolworth's full potential. The insurance companies, pension funds, unit trusts and other institutions who backed the 1982 buy-out did so on the basis that it would take seven years to accomplish that task. But if Dixons had been willing to nudge their bid from £1.8 billion to £2 billion it would have been difficult for those fund managers to justify to their trustees that they should give Woolworth the benefit of the doubt. As it was, only the determined loyalty of Prudential Assurance and the Merchant Navy pension fund thwarted Dixons and allowed Woolworth to fight on as an independent entity.

Whittaker is convinced that Dixons launched its attack when it did only because there were distinct signs that the breakthrough was beginning to happen. Woolworth's profits had been stuck at around £40 million since 1982, but for the year to the end of January 1986 the figure suddenly jumped to £60 million. 'They realised we'd cracked it,' said Whittaker.

What the post-1982 management had cracked was the problem, big enough in itself, of imposing up-to-date financial controls, slashing stock levels and overheads, and selling unprofitable stores in rundown areas. 'The first year after the takeover from the Americans was spent putting in some basic controls and sorting out what we had got,' explained Mulcahy, a Geordie with a degree in physics and chemistry who cut his teeth at Esso before joining British Sugar, and now Woolworth's chief executive. 'We had to create order out of chaos, because the group was rapidly haemorrhaging.' What was left to be done, and what Dixons' chairman, Stanley Kalms, claimed his team could do much better, was to develop a new retailing strategy.

The ace up Woolworth's sleeve was B & Q, the DIY chain which the former management had been castigated for buying. Mulcahy admits that they poured money into B & Q because it could be expanded quickly and produce profits while they got down to disentangling the Woolies chain.

'B & Q gave us time to work on the Woolworths chain,' Whittaker explained. 'We see B & Q as the monster in the middle of the DIY sector, pushing everyone else into specialising. It is the biggest in Europe, and the biggest garden centre chain in Europe. B & Q's objective is to have the best DIY range, along with kitchens, bathrooms, carpets, and builders' merchants, which is an area that has not been attacked properly by retailers. That is also true of car parts, which we are also going into through Autocentres. They sell car parts, accessories, give advice, service and a car wash. We have invested a lot into B & Q's electronic point-of-sale system. It helps us to cut stock, change prices more quickly and order faster.'

Woolworth's other out-of-town name is Comet, the cut-price electrical goods chain taken over for £177 million in 1984. This stretched the group management even further, because it did not intend to make a move for Comet until at least a year later. But it was do or die, there and then, after Sir Phil Harris's Harris

Dixons: busy, aggressive, product-led.

Boots the Chemist in a Cardiff shopping centre.

The funfair comes to town at Childrens World.

Woolworths before the War, and new releases at Woolworths in 1987.

Queensway made a bid. It is the biggest out of town electrical retailer, and second or third in electrical retailing overall. The main thrust of Comet is to have big out-of-town locations and low rents.

But even so, Comet needed fine-tuning. 'Comet's strategy didn't fit in with the strategy of the producers, especially the Japanese,' said Mulcahy. 'They didn't want to be associated with a cutprice discounter, but we are rebuilding those relationships, sometimes by giving away extra goods like video tapes or calculators rather than cutting prices. Comet were buying cheap, a little like the old Woolworths. It's all right at first, when the suppliers are themselves just getting started and they are glad of all the orders they can get. But this cowboy image doesn't work once the suppliers develop a strategy.'

The strategy at Woolworth was to develop a chain of chains. The business was honed into six specialist areas: kids, gifts and sweets, entertainment, home and garden, kitchenshop, and looks. This was the master plan known as Operation Focus. By focusing on these areas, so the theory went, Woolworth would have a clearer identity and could hope to be the market leader, or thereabouts, in each case. Mulcahy explained: 'We dropped food because its margins were too low and adult clothing because we were not going to be as good as Burton or Next.'

The new layout is being displayed through two types of store, Weekend and General. The Weekend stores are 20-40,000 sq ft with displays set off at angles to encourage shoppers to browse before taking their choices to central cash desks. They are in locations where there is easy comparison with direct competitors such as Marks & Spencer, W H Smith or Our Price. The General Stores are smaller, more like convenience stores, with very little comparison shopping nearby.

The intention is that if the new plan works it will be expanded to the point where a whole shop will be given over to each of the six specialist areas. 'We have opened a shop called Kidstore, just with that one department there. If it works, we may do it with the other units,' said Mulcahy.

The result is that Woolworth Holdings, the main board of the company, now sees itself as running a group of retail businesses, of which the Woolworths chain is only one, and others may be added as and when the opportunities arise. 'We want to develop a portfolio of retailing names,' Mulcahy explained. 'We want a situation where some are coming through and producing good profits, so that we can use the money to grow new businesses. Our future is in having commercial trading companies, all with a clear sense of direction.'

The head office has now detached itself from Woolworth's long-standing headquarters in London's Marylebone Road. They have taken a small office across the road, with a modest entrance sandwiched between a branch of Royal Bank of Scotland and Town and Country Building Society. The extent to which this core team gets involved with the individual shop chains depends on the state of each business. They each have to have a five-year plan, an annual budget, monthly and weekly reporting and capital expenditure budgets. And they also want to know what is being done to develop new management talent.

They decide how to allocate resources to each operation by getting a strategy agreed with each of their managements, and that determines where the money is going over the next three or four years. The main criterion is, understandably, the return each can make on the investment sunk in it. But they must have a commercial strategy. 'The thing that drives us is return on capital,' said Mulcahy. 'If pretty stores do that, fine; if not, forget it. We have got to have a good merchandise offer. Design has to support that, not the other way round.'

Mulcahy and Whittaker give a clear impression that they feel underrated, and are at pains to stress that to the best of their belief they are one of the fastest growing retail concerns in the country. Their soreness on this point was not helped by the allegation during the Dixons struggle that they were not even entitled to be called retailers. This bizarre claim can be understood only in terms of the distinction between those who have been in the business all their lives, starting off as speckled youths behind shop counters, and those who have come into it in a management role as they would any other industry.

Mulcahy, who spent two years at Harvard Business School, is scathing about those who pride themselves on their ability to fly by the seat of their pants. 'Most other retailing companies are run by people who have grown up with the business.' he said. 'They have put a formula together which happens to have worked, and that is why they have survived and prospered. But the big change that is taking place in the high street is that the winners are going to be those businesses that have actually got a good strategic management backed by a pretty good executive management. A lot of retailers don't know why they are successful. But if you don't know that you can't adapt to change, and that is going to be more and more essential in future.'

It is hard to fault Woolworth for its efforts to adapt to the retailing revolution. But, like Boots and W H Smith, it will be some time before it can claim to have pulled off what will be a remarkable escape from the edge of the abyss.

Fireside Shopping

THE PROTAGONISTS:
- GREAT UNIVERSAL STORES
- EMPIRE STORES

Mail order is a corner of retailing that has long been neglected, but now seems about to be pushed into centre stage. It has suffered from being the traditional preserve of poorer shoppers, pouring over bulky catalogues in their front parlours. But that is changing. The colour magazines given away with Sunday newspapers have projected a more affluent image, carrying advertisements offering luxury goods by phone, payable with a credit card. The credit card companies themselves have built on that idea by sending mini-catalogues with their monthly bills. Suddenly, mail order is becoming respectable, even fashionable.

In its present-day form, mail order first caught on in the United States in the 1880s, as a means of overcoming long distances to reach people living in out-of-the-way places. But its early stirrings were seen in Britain in the clubs that were set up to enable consumers to buy goods they could not otherwise afford. The progenitor of that idea, oddly enough, was the eighteenth-century building society.

As the chapter on Halifax Building Society explains, the seeds were sown when groups of craftsmen banded together to buy materials and build houses for one another. Lots were drawn to see who should have each house as it was completed. The same thing happened in the 1850s when John Fattorini, part of a family of Italian immigrants based in Bradford, started the first Fattorini Watch Club.

Until recently, the mail order groups had their hands full extending their original principle of bringing new goods, from prams to televisions, within reach of people who could not pay for them in one lump and wanted the convenience of choosing in their own homes, or meeting friends to discuss the latest catalogue. By the so-called agency system, one person registers as an agent, receives the catalogue and persuades friends to buy from it. The company pays the agent ten per cent commission. Direct mail order has become more popular lately, whereby each shopper has his or her own catalogue, often sent in response to a coupon cut from an advertisement, and orders from it without any commission being involved.

Hire purchase sprang up in the 1950s to offer a rival instalment system, but it was largely confined to bulky durables like washing machines. And the shops that used HP had to cover the overheads on their high street premises, a cost that mail order avoided.

Because they tended to sell the more expensive items, as living standards rose mail order captured a bigger and bigger share of the overall retail market. But in the early 1980s it began to fall behind. By 1981 mail order's share of all mixed and non-food retailing was less than six per cent. A growing proportion of the population found they had all they needed by way of consumer goods, and could increasingly pay for replacements by credit card. Spare cash was going on holidays and entertainment, and of course the high street was beginnning to respond to a public that was more willing to be titillated into buying what it might be persuaded into wanting, rather than merely what it needed.

The mail order houses have reacted in two directions, both mirroring what has been happening in the shops. All retailers have eagerly embraced computers as a source of stock control and market research, but the advances in computerisation have been far more valuable in mail order. The difference is that mail order firms have far more information about their customers, their likes and dislikes and where they live. This has given them the chance to move in another direction, targeting their audiences more precisely, as the high street chains have been doing.

Freemans, the London mail order firm, was the first in Britain to go into specialised catalogues, or 'specialogs', as they are known across the Atlantic. There has since been a rash of these slimline books, covering women of most ages and sizes, mothers and babies, do-it-yourself, the elderly. The hunt is on for more and more targets, as long as they cover enough people to make it worth printing 100,000 catalogues.

But while the traditional mail order houses have been busily bringing themselves up to date, a new threat has appeared over the horizon. In 1986 Grattan, which had been formed by another branch of the Fattorini family, was taken over by Next.

George Davies, the boss of Next, is determined to take the high street by storm with his designer-led concept which can be adapted into almost any type of retailing. It was logical that he should apply his theories to mail order, or home shopping as he prefers to call it. And when he bought Grattan he acquired a powerful and talented lieutenant. Grattan's chief executive is David Jones, who learnt his trade at Great Universal Stores, the group assembled by Sir Isaac Wolfson and UK mail order's dominant force.

There has always been a tension between the high street and the catalogue in retailing. It has even produced a hybrid, Argos, which manages to combine the two. Several groups over the years, including Empire and for that matter GUS, have run the two operations in tandem. However, Empire sold its shops many years ago and GUS does not try to cross-fertilize the two in the public's mind. Burberry, Scotch House, Hector Powe and Lennards shops are not openly linked with the Great Universal, Kay's or John Myers catalogues.

Davies and Jones, who could turn into one of retailing's legendary double acts if they stay together long enough, appear to have none of these inhibitions. They want to use the Next name to seduce their high street customers into taking Next catalogues home and picking up the phone.

Both Habitat and Mothercare, under the wing of Sir Terence Conran, have long published in-store catalogues. But without the warehousing and distribution infrastructure they have not been able to make the jump into mail order. Until a few years ago it probably would not have worked anyway. The typical upwardly mobile Habitat customer would have shied away from buying by mail order because that was the sort of thing his or her parents had done in their two up-two down back home.

Burton Group also toyed with mail order, but gave it up as a bad job in 1971 after seven years of struggle. It is an undeniably hard trade to break into, because it takes expensive time to build up a mailing list of regular and creditworthy spenders. Davies has leapfrogged that hurdle by buying an existing business, and one that had already spent heavily on computer systems.

Win or lose, Next is likely to give the rest of the mail order the competitive spur it needs to maintain its share of consumer spending. That is going to require innovation and imagination, coupled with more efficient delivery systems. People do not meet in a pub every week for a year any more just so that they can buy a watch. They are more likely to sit at home, pick up the phone, put a video catalogue on the TV, and order a crate of wine.

THE GREAT UNIVERSAL PROVIDER

Great Universal Stores, inevitably known in the trade as GUS, is the undisputed leader of Britain's mail order industry. Like Marks & Spencer, it rarely innovates and is cautious about jumping on rivals' bandwagons, but when it strikes out in a new direction it does so with a thoroughness which can pierce the toughest competition.

Although the company began life at the turn of the century as a Manchester mail order firm called Universal Stores, in its modern form it is substantially the creation of Sir Isaac Wolfson, a Glaswegian who joined the company in 1932 at the age of 35 and was chairman from 1946 until 1986. He is now honorary life president and his son, Lord Wolfson, is the present Chairman. Sir Isaac and Lord Wolfson are trustees of the Wolfson Foundation and other charitable trusts which together speak for 49.9 of GUS's voting shares. The two men own another 1.6 per cent of the shares personally, giving them effective control of the group when all these stakes are combined.

Today GUS sells through a number of catalogues including Great Universal, Marshall Ward, John England, John Noble, John Myers, Family Album, Kays and Kit. Kays is based in Worcester and was taken over in 1937. But from the 1940s GUS spread out into the high street. Under Sir Isaac's leadership it bought chains of stores specialising in furniture, clothing and do-it-yourself, both in the UK and abroad, and it expanded into mail order in Austria, Holland, Sweden and Switzerland. It went into travel with Global Holidays and gradually developed a finance and property operation to channel the profits of the mainstream businesses.

Those profits have risen each year without a break since 1950 as Sir Isaac and his son have expanded the business to the point where the group commands over forty per cent of the mail order trade in Britain. It has more than three million agents, each of whom has an average of two and a half customers, spread around the country and throughout the social spectrum.

Recently GUS has been retrenching. In 1985 it sold Global Travel to International Leisure, the Intasun package holiday concern, and the following year Harris Queensway bought

Thoms Household Stores, Times Furnishing and Home Charm from the group. It still has a restricted and rather exclusive high street presence through Burberrys and the Scotch House as well as the Lennards shoe shop chain, but now more than at any time in the past forty years GUS is concentrating on its heartland – mail order, finance and property.

Among the spinoffs from mail order is the fastest-growing part of the group. It goes under the anonymous-sounding name of CCN Systems, but it plays an important part in the expansion of GUS's mail-order operations whilst earning useful profits by hiring its talents to any other business that wants them.

Those talents add up to the ability to handle, sift and process vast amounts of information for market research, credit-checking and company searches. CCN was formed only in 1980 with a staff of 100 who dealt with three million enquiries in that first year. Now it employs 2,000 people who cope with an annual 25 million enquiries in what is believed to be Britain's largest computerised information business. More than forty million names and addresses sit in the CCN computers, together with County Court judgements and bankruptcy records, and information on more than two million companies, partnerships and sole traders. The more businesses want to offer credit, the more they need access to a database which can help them make up their minds about who are the good and bad payers.

GUS reckons it is learning to use the database more selectively, refining its techniques of credit scoring and credit performance. The company used to send a man round to the local grocer to find out how a prospective customer had been doing. The trick is to balance higher volume against higher bad debts. If it rises they tighten the credit scoring. GUS now thinks it is ahead of its American competition in that respect. The US started credit scoring, but GUS now has a majority holding in a credit scoring company over there, and has put its own people in to improve it.

CCN has three main divisions – direct marketing, consumer credit and business information. The first rents the forty million names and addresses, but so that firms can sell as economically as possible the forty million can be divided according to age, sex, social class and geography to fit any marketing profile. The consumer credit service enables those same firms to look more closely at those who respond to an offer, to see who is likely to be creditworthy. In each case the firm using the service makes the commercial judgment based on the information CCN supplies. The business information division provides the same sort of service in respect of companies rather than individuals.

GUS says: 'CCN Systems is a major provider of business services in the UK – services which contribute directly to the profitability and market penetration of its client organisations.' And CCN's biggest client is, of course, its parent – GUS.

That back-up has become invaluable in helping GUS to follow the trend towards more precisely targeted marketing. Specialised catalogues have become the buzzword in the last two or three years. They are target marketed at sections of the population, and CCN undoubtedly helps. It does not mean the demise of the 1,000-page catalogue yet, but the strength of a specialised catalogue is its identity with a target audience. Publishing a DIY catalogue is better than sending a 1,000-page catalogue and hoping that the DIY enthusiasts will turn up the DIY section. CCN gives GUS the socio-economic groupings for a catalogue like Fashion Extra, aimed at women of size 16 and over. GUS can use its database to send the catalogues to the top 100,000 agents in sales of particular merchandise or by residential classification.

Mail order is following the high street in the designer concept. And GUS is going upmarket. The group claims ten per cent of the ABs, the country's top socio-economic categories. The consumer has been gradually switching from low prices to the subtly different concept of value for money. That gives a group like GUS the scope for an increase in unit prices if it can persuade people to perceive better quality and better value.

Technological advances have been important to GUS, not only in computerising information, but also in streamlining the biggest cost headache for any mail order house, warehousing and distribution. The company has been able to take full advantage of this because of its size, and has led the way in this direction. At the end of March 1986 GUS was committed to capital spending of nearly £23 million, a figure which small firms have difficulty matching.

Lots of people at GUS used to be employed in what is known as picking and packing, but now much of the hard work of sorting and retrieving goods for dispatch goes through computerised equipment. A large percentage of sales are done on the telephone now. The telephone girls have access to the agent's account on the computer, so a telephonist can tell immediately whether something has been dispatched. The colour and size of an item can be agreed on the phone, cutting the expensive business of handling returned goods from dissatisfied customers.

Nine out of every ten GUS parcels travel on the company's White Arrow fleet of lorries, as well as many of the returns. But GUS still claims to have the largest contract of anyone with the Post Office. Half the orders from customers come through the post and small packages go out through that route.

Mail order is becoming more popular as town centres become more choked, parking becomes more difficult and people want increasing leisure time and do not want to give time to shopping. But the merchandise has to be as good as the illustrations of it in the catalogue. That is a problem that has become more apparent as GUS, like the other mail order houses, trades up to attract a more affluent and inevitably more demanding breed of customer.

It is one of the details that Sir Phil Harris of Harris Queensway is likely to have pertinent views about. His arrival as a non-executive director on the GUS board in July 1986 signalled that GUS may be poised for fresh developments. His appointment was connected with Harris Queensway's purchase of part of GUS's high street operations, in return for which GUS acquired a 23 per cent stake in HQ.

Neither GUS nor Sir Phil made any public comment on the implications of the link-up at the time, but the move was seen by outside commentators as a way of bringing Sir Phil's retail expertise to bear on GUS as Sir Isaac Wolfson's reign drew to a close. John Richards, the widely respected retail analyst at the stockbrokers Wood Mackenzie, remarked: 'Since GUS is totally lacking in entrepreneurial flair, it is clear that Sir Philip has all the makings of an heir apparent for GUS.' And the *Financial Times* added: 'The question now for Sir Philip and the Wolfson family is just how close their future relationship should become. A merger of the two companies, with Sir Philip eventually taking over at the top, looks a distinct possibility.'

GUS has the enviable problem of ensuring enough cutting edge to retain leadership in a branch of retailing that has been going through its own special revolution, strongly influenced by high street trends but with the additional challenge of harnessing computer power to reach and deliver to the customer accurately and efficiently.

The Next takeover of Grattan showed how the high street shop and the mail order catalogue are coming closer together. Whereas the consumer used to be faced with the dilemma of leafing through a catalogue at home or spending possibly a couple of hours trudging to the nearest shopping centre, the car has become for many the mobile home extension that has brought the shops nearer to everyone's front door. Traffic, parking and bad weather will always be a deterrent, but against that has to be balanced the attraction of wider choice.

The computer is beginning to help mail order in another way: by replacing the catalogue with video tapes illustrating the goods, and enabling customers to place orders electronically. GUS has a remarkable record of adapting to change, and more than ever it will be able to argue that retailing is becoming a seamless robe as the various ways of reaching the consumer merge and overlap with one another.

THE ITALIAN EMPIRE

The romantic legend of Empire Stores is that it owes its origins to Antonio Fattorini, who was said to have been born in 1797 in the Lombardy village of Bellagio on Lake Como. He joined the Duke of Wellington's army during the Napoleonic Wars, but arrived in Belgium just too late for the Battle of Waterloo. When the army was disbanded he came to Dewsbury in Yorkshire and began life as a pedlar.

The evidence for this story is scanty, although Fattorini is a common name in the Lombardy region. What is known is that after several years on the road in England Antonio rented a stall in the newly-established Briggate Market, Leeds, in 1827, and took a lease on a shop in the market four years later.

His pedlar's trade had naturally led him into jewellery and

fancy goods, and these were what he stocked in his shop. That was to have an important bearing on the family's eventual move into mail order. And it was because he was dealing in luxuries that he opened a branch in Harrogate, then as now an affluent town which had been identified as such by Marshall & Snelgrove and Debenhams, two smart London stores which had gone to the trouble of opening branches there. What was good enough for them was good enough for Antonio Fattorini, he decided.

His next move proved to be historically important. He opened a shop in Bradford, the home of Empire Stores today. It was a prosperous town, plugged into the new canal and railway systems, with a longstanding worsted manufacturing tradition to support it and iron and coal industries nearby.

The Fattorini family grew and expanded. Antonio had seven sons, who went into the business and set up shops of their own, although they bought centrally to take advantage of bulk discounts. It was John, the youngest son, who had the idea of forming Watch Clubs which would save up for watches until every member had one.

It worked like this. The Fattorinis would go round the pubs and encourage the locals to form a club, complete with chairman, secretary and treasurer. Each member would chip in 6d (2½p) a week into the club. When the kitty reached £1 5s (£1.25) the money was sent to a Fattorini jewellery shop to buy a silver pocket watch. After the chairman had shown the watch round the pub it was raffled among the members. Everyone, winners and losers, kept paying in their subscriptions until they had a watch each.

Watches were chosen at first because there was a growing need for them in industry. Every railway employee had to have one, but they cost the equivalent of a week's wages. Few retailers wanted to give credit to the people who found they needed them to get a job. The club system shielded the Fattorinis from bad debts, for slow payers had to be chased by the clubs themselves. They fined the laggards, and that paid for a club dinner every so often.

By the time everyone in a particular club had a watch, the club had become something of a social institution and an excuse for a weekly pint with friends. So after the watches had all been distributed they looked around for something else to buy – a set of cutlery or a table clock. Eventually the Fattorinis short-circuited the process by simply sending the club a cheque for the appropriate sum, so that the winner of each draw could spend it how he liked . . . except that the cheque was valid only in a Fattorini shop.

Some of these clubs were in pubs tucked away in the more remote parts of the Yorkshire dales, so the Fattorinis took to posting the goods. As tastes grew more sophisticated, the shops' range was brought together in a catalogue so that the lucky club member could choose from the entire stock. Mail order was born. In 1910, after the Americans had turned it into a thoroughgoing industry, the Fattorinis founded Empire Stores, still one of Britain's leading mail order houses.

This was the precursor of mail order, in that the concept incorporated the features of instalment payments and orders generated with minimal use of the retailer's staff and premises. Bad debts were non-existent, because the watches were handed over by the Fattorinis only when they had received the money. The social element was there, too. Just like today's Tupperware parties and the groups of friends meeting to discuss a mail order catalogue over a cup of tea, the Watch Clubs were social gatherings in pubs, where inevitably much of the conversation turned to the Fattorinis' products. What more could a retailer ask?

It was the social adhesive which made it possible for the family to extend into the modern form of mail order. That meant going down market, offering clothes, blankets, and shoes as well as jewellery. It also meant handing over the goods after the first instalment payment instead of the last. Saving up for a watch was one thing, but the new customers could not afford to wait twenty weeks or more for a household necessity. So the club system was replaced by a network of agents, who were responsible for picking customers who would not let them down. 'All of a sudden Bradford was full of agents,' a young lad of the time recalled. 'Everywhere you went, mills and workrooms had one.' They were also at the pitheads and in the pubs. It was quite a craze.

For families living on £1.50 a week, nearly half of which went on food and rent, the new means of paying for the more expensive items opened the way to a higher standard of living. The Fattorinis followed their customers into the leisure age, selling sports clothes, equipment, trophies and medals. The present Football Association cup is a Fattorini product, won for the first time in 1911, appropriately enough by Bradford City.

So successful was the mail order business that it was formed into a separate company in 1910, called Empire Stores. But within two years there was a family split and Enrico Fattorini went to another part of Bradford to set up Grattan Warehouses. Both duly became leaders in their field, and it was the same Grattan which was taken over in 1986 by Next.

Up to the Second World War the mail order houses kept the loyalty of their traditional working class customer base and expanded their range of products. But they were unattractive, unbranded goods. Then there was meteoric growth after the war, when there was a great improvement in standards of living. Mail order grew with that improvement. For thirty years, from 1950 to 1980, mail order's share of retail sales increased every year, except for years when there was a postal strike. Even the incomes policies of the Wilson and Heath governments helped the traditional mail order customers. Six per cent or £3 a week was a better pay rise than many of them had seen in their lives, and it narrowed the differentials between the poorest-paid workers and those further up the ladder.

But Empire was hit harder than any of the other major mail order houses by the recession which began to bite in 1980. Rising unemployment blighted the northern industrial areas which form Empire's heartland. Bad debts and postal costs soared, and Empire could not match the bulk buying power of the market leaders, Great Universal Stores and Littlewoods. Empire plunged from profits of £7.7 million in the year to the end of January 1979 to £1.1 million loss four years later.

It was a crisis that in December 1981 led the Empire board of directors to cast around for an alliance with one of the bigger mail order houses. The business jungle being what it is, the price of that alliance was almost certain to be Empire's independence. That, at any rate, was the condition imposed by GUS, who would give Empire the help it needed only when GUS had taken over the ailing business. Empire's directors agreed, subject to GUS giving assurances that it would keep the Empire business separate and not create any 'material' redundancies. But of course, once GUS had legal control of Empire it would be bound to do whatever was necessary in the interests of its shareholders as a whole.

Quite what GUS would have done we shall never know, because the Government asked the Monopolies and Mergers Commission to investigate the planned deal. The Commission not only concluded that the merger would be against the public interest, it recommended that GUS should be ordered to cut its share stake in Empire from 29.9 per cent to under ten per cent so that the way would be clear for other organisations to link up with Empire or even to take it over.

The Commission objected to the merger because GUS already had forty per cent of the mail order market in the UK, and Empire would have added another seven per cent. The two companies argued unsuccessfully that what should be measured was their share of the retail market as a whole, of which mail order was only a part, because the mail order houses had to compete with the shops for custom. That cut no ice. The Commission's report said: 'GUS is the dominant company in a distinct sector of a market which is particularly difficult to enter and which is already characterised by an unusually high degree of concentration.'

So Empire was left to soldier on. Sears and one or two others talked to them about merging, but nothing came of it. Instead, Empire attracted friendly shareholdings from two companies, Vendex International of the Netherlands and the Italian-based Gecos, who each acquired a twenty per cent stake. GUS reduced its holding, but by 1986 had rebuilt it to 12.7 per cent of the shares.

Meanwhile, Empire set about streamlining its operations. Bigger and more powerful computers were wheeled in to identify and sift customers, and to speed the ordering and restocking process. In-house credit-rating rules were tightened to crack down on customers who were likely to be slow payers or outright bilkers. By the 1986 year-end, profits had recovered to £5.8 million.

Peter Fattorini, Empire's marketing director and the only remaining member of the founding family on the board, claimed: 'In recent years mail order has got its own house in order and started to produce goods people want.' As mail order companies are the only retailers who never see their customers in the ordinary course of events, they have turned to extensive market research to bridge the gap.

Even more than other types of retailing, mail order demands that decisions be backed heavily for months or even years before they can be expected to pay off. The range of goods has to be chosen and priced in good time for the all-important catalogues to be designed. Mail order houses do not have shopkeepers' high street overheads, but neither do they have their flexibility.

'New customers make no money for us in the first year, or even two years, because of the cost of getting them through the door,' said Fattorini. 'We recruit people for the catalogue through advertising, and we might get 10,000 coupons back from one advertisement. Of those between 2,500 and 4,000 will buy something, and to encourage them we send them a gift like a hair dryer with their first purchase. So it can cost between £25 and £30 to get a new customer on that basis, by the time you allow for the cost of advertising. They will spend only about £50 each on average in the first season, and there is a very high dropout rate. After three years you are down to maybe 1,000 from the original 10,000. Only then are that 1,000 generating revenue for the company. Of course you can improve profits by cutting spending on recruiting new agents and customers, but at the risk of losing out on future revenue.'

Meanwhile the average number of customers per catalogue has fallen from fourteen to two. This is partly because more catalogues have been distributed as the big firms have fought to poach one another's agents and customers. There are now 6.5 million mail order catalogues circulating in Britain at any one time, roughly one for every three households.

That has inevitably led Empire and its rivals into more precise targeting, taking a cue from the high street trend in that same direction. Empire began by launching three separate, tightly targeted catalogues. The first was 010, aimed at children up to ten years and maternity wear. That was followed by Complete Comfort, aimed officially at people over 45, but in practice for older people and selling woolly and thermal underwear, security products, specially designed garden tools and waterproof clothes. The third targeted catalogue was Elements, a fashion catalogue for that much sought-after creature, the 20-35 year old woman, selling good value co-ordinated and not too extreme fashion. It is no coincidence that that sounds uncannily like the Next blueprint.

'Until now we have had a lot of shallow ranges selling a wide range of goods, but just a little of each,' said Fattorini. 'Specialist catalogues enable us to offer a range in depth. In all cases we are aiming to get people from outside those who would normally buy the big catalogues and would anyway not buy enough from the big catalogue. We can pick them out from our computer, and we rent lists.'

Empire has had to come to terms with the fact that mail order's four traditional strengths, the four Cs of credit, convenience, commission and a comprehensive range have gradually become less relevant. A dwindling band rely on commission to supplement their income, but credit and comprehensive ranges are as readily available in the high street. Mail order can still offer convenience to those who have neither the time nor the inclination to go shopping, but it must continually prove itself efficient and responsive to the increasingly rapid shifts in tastes.

If Empire is to survive as an independent force it will have to return to its roots and develop more specialist niches for itself in order to avoid competing against the enormous buying power wielded by GUS and Littlewoods, and the threat posed by the Next-Grattan combination.

Money for the Asking

THE PROTAGONISTS:
- NATIONAL WESTMINSTER BANK
- THE HALIFAX BUILDING SOCIETY

While some retailers have been packing their bags and moving out of town, and many of the old independent shopkeepers have reluctantly closed in the face of competition from the big battalions, vacant high street sites have been snapped up by providers of financial services. In some towns, like Bournemouth, whole streets have been taken over by banks and building societies. They have also moved into shopping centres, for the same reason that they find the high street so attractive: to catch the passing trade with window displays offering ever more alluring ways to save and borrow.

At one time, financial services were the preserve of the rich. They were the only people with spare money to invest, and they were the only people worth lending to. But as standards of living have grown, and more sophisticated methods of checking people's creditworthiness have developed, so the retail financial market has mushroomed.

Now seventy per cent of adults in Britain have a bank account and, in the words of Seymour Fortescue, a general manager of Barclays, 'the remaining unbanked are probably unbankable', either because they prefer using cash or they are too feckless to run a bank account without running into difficulties.

Traditionally, people were nudged into their parents' bank or chose the nearest one. Parental influence may have waned, though branch location is still a vital weapon in the battle for new customers. But in the past decade the main impetus for opening bank accounts has come from employers understandably wishing to avoid the greater risk of theft arising from having to pay employees in cash every week. That has been a marketing bonus for the banks, as it fits in neatly with a radical change in their own priorities.

The macho end of banking always used to be mega-loans to nations and corporations. But most of the big banks have had to write off millions of pounds lent to third world countries, and the competition to lend to companies is extremely tough. While corporate lending will continue to provide the banks' bread and butter because of its scale, the high street is becoming more interesting for its apparently easier pickings. Regulations are being dismantled, and the consumer is becoming richer and more attuned to borrowing. Once 'debt' was a dirty word, but now it is known as 'credit' and has become positively respectable.

The personal sector is rapidly becoming as competitive as the corporate sector in banking. The current account is now a loss leader as competition has forced the banks to give up charging for this facility if the account is kept in credit. So they can make money only by lending, selling insurance and dealing in investments such as unit trusts and stocks and shares for their customers.

Sadly from their point of view, the banks do not have a captive audience for these profitable lines of business. The big five – Barclays, Lloyds, Midland, National Westminster and the Trustee Savings Bank – naturally compete with one another. Employees tend to be ushered through the doors of their employer's bank if they have not already got an account. When banking was a more gentlemanly pastime they all used to sit back and rely on fate to deliver them their fair share of such random trade. Not any more. The banks are devoting enormous time and effort to ensnaring children, so that by the time they have a job they will have a ready-made bank account. Advertising and promotion have helped to make the customer more fickle than before, and children are the most fickle of all.

And the competition no longer stops there. Retailers have realised that their customers often need to borrow to pay for the goods they see in the shops. In the years running up to its takeover by Burton Group in 1985, Debenhams regularly used to make more money from lending than from shopkeeping. Harris Queensway, the group which takes in Times Furnishing, Carpetland, Electric Supreme, Poundstretcher and Hamleys, has launched its own credit card, Impact, which it hopes will eventually rank third in the country behind Visa and Access. And then there are the building societies.

In the fight to dominate the financial end of the high street, everyone else is stealing sidelong glances at the building societies. Long regarded as the sleeping giant of the financial services industry, the home loans movement is waking up with a vengeance that frightens their competitors. Their most potent asset is the goodwill with which they are regarded by the public, an asset they are now beginning to draw on in earnest, thanks to a change in the law with effect from January 1987. The new law enables them to lend more freely than before, and to offer other services.

Just as the banks have happily muscled into the societies' territory by offering mortgages, so the big societies are now hitting back with plastic cards and perhaps chequebooks – although they have noticed how cheques have become something of a penance for the banks and are happy to let them keep that burden to themselves. But otherwise the two sectors are in the process becoming more alike, at least as far as financial retailing is concerned.

By one of those quirks that is not entirely coincidental, about seventy per cent of homes in Britain are owned by their occupiers, the overwhelming proportion of whom must take out a mortgage to finance the purchase, and indeed are advised to do so to benefit from tax relief. As the same number of people have mortgages as have bank accounts, both markets are close to saturation point.

That can only make the competition fiercer. Computerisation has brought down the cost of transmitting money, so the deals on offer are becoming more attractive. but it is a business in which it is notoriously difficult to keep a competitive edge, because as soon as someone comes out with a good idea there is nothing to stop everyone else from copying it.

That is in turn making many financial retailers less fussy about who they take on as customers. At one time it used to take a standard six months of impeccable behaviour before a new bank account holder could qualify for a cheque card. But that seems a shade harsh, as cheques without a card are now virtually unusable unless you are using them to pay a friend, or are actually drawing your own money out of the bank.

So the race is on to cut the qualifying period. By the end of 1986 the TSB had it down to two weeks. Their rivals scornfully argued that that will earn the TSB only the riskier type of customer, but the same derision was voiced when the Midland led the way with free banking for those in credit. They all eventually fell into line, and the pattern is likely to be repeated with cheque card waiting time.

The same sort of thing is happening to interest rates. No one, bank or building society or department store, dare be out of line for too long lest they be either inundated or left high and dry, depending on whether they are leading the crowd or are behind it.

The members of the Building Societies Association used to operate a cartel whereby they fixed the principal mortgage and deposit rates at a monthly meeting. But the Abbey and some of the other big societies felt strong enough to buck the cartel, and tried to hold the queue for mortgages at a manageable level by adjusting the interest rate. Rationing by price, it was called. But the banks put an end to that game when they entered the mortgage market and started undercutting the societies. Now, instead of a queue of borrowers there is a queue of lenders.

The trouble is that as a result the margin between what financial groups pay to attract funds and what they charge to lend is being whittled to the point where there is a danger that they will not make money out of it. That has already happened to current account charges. If it happens to lending, everyone in the business will have to move on to some other activity to make money. Then competition will take the profit margin out of that, and they will have to move on to something else, and so on. It is a merry-go-round that will have to stop somewhere, or the providers of these sevices will begin to go out of business. And that will do customers no good at all.

THE ACTION BANK TURNS PIGGY BANK

If someone stopped you in the street and asked if you wanted to borrow some money, you would be right to wonder what the catch was. But nowadays such a person might be one of National Westminster's 'street bankers' trying to pick up a likely-looking customer. It is a far cry from the days when people had to crave an appointment with the local manager to seek a loan, and mind their P's and Q's while they were about it. NatWest got the idea from New York, where bankers drum up business on the streets of Harlem. The British bank hit on it as a way of helping new businesses to get started in the worst inner-city areas after the 1981 riots.

Officially called Business Development Officers, NatWest's street bankers walk the streets and frequent the clubs of places like Toxteth or Handsworth searching for people who might feel uncomfortable about walking into a bank branch, but who have ideas which can be turned into projects worth lending money on. It is a way of bridging the age, language, racial and cultural gaps between one of Britain's biggest banks and communities who regard them as pillars of the white Anglo-Saxon establishment. The after-sales service includes keeping in touch to help these new borrowers through the difficult early stages of launching a business.

Naturally, not all the new projects succeed, and not all the areas overcome their natural hostility to someone they see as trying to make money out of them. But it has created jobs and it has created businesses, some of which might grow into substantial and enduring enterprises – and it has done no harm to NatWest's self-proclaimed image as The Action Bank. Above all, the very idea of such a venture shows how the face of retail banking has changed in the past decade or so.

Nowadays the name of the game is to get 'em in through the door at almost any cost, on the assumption that enough people will turn into borrowers, unit trust investors, insurance policy-holders or home buyers to make it worth NatWest's while. The first and most obvious target was university students, who have a grant to bank and better job prospects than most.

NatWest has since gone down the age range, to the point where it recruits children as young as a year old who are eligible to receive Woody, a ceramic baby piglet complete with nappy, as soon as they have put £3 in their Piggy Bank Account – or had it opened for them by a doting relative. There are four more in the family, Annabel, Maxwell, Lady Hilary and Sir Nathaniel Westminster, all given away free one by one as the young savers leave another £25 in their account over a period of at least two years. More than a million of these porky figures have been issued, implying that the scheme has attracted around £25 million. Not bad out of pocket money and presents from parents, aunts and uncles.

To cover the ages between ankle socks and college scarves NatWest has an account called On Line. Teenagers collect a brightly coloured folder, year planner, address and phone book, wallet and pocket calculator, together with a four-monthly magazine. If they are over fourteen they qualify for a Servicecard to withdraw up to £25 from the bank's hole-in-the-wall machines.

'Teenagers are the most difficult to get through to,' said Derek Wanless, NatWest's director of personal banking services, 'but On Line has been successful. Children's accounts are highly fashionable: because of all the promotions and special offers they are the most multi-banked part of the market. That is why the Piggies have worked so well, because they encourage the children to build up and stay with that one account. The problem there is the age range. We have Piggy Bank account holders from one year old to eighteen. It makes it very hard to write their magazine! The point is that people used to come to us only when there was a definite need, a first salary cheque or a student grant. Now we are getting them younger. And they are not put off by banks any more. In fact they like it, because they can show their friends that they have joined the adult world.'

The pressure for banks to catch their customers young has been intensified by the shift towards free banking as long as an account is in credit. This was started by one or two of the regional banks in an effort to lure business away from their bigger brothers. And, starting with the Midland, the big banks have all had to fall into line or wave bye-bye to thousands of customers. Although 'free' banking has saved the banks' money by slowing the merry-go-round of constantly having to open and close accounts, it has made the banks all the keener to sell their other services, for until they do they are not earning a penny from the people who walk in through their doors. It also happens to be good psychology: people are far more touchy about paying a few pounds in bank charges on a current account than perhaps twenty-six per cent annual interest on a loan.

'All most borrowers are concerned about is how much the monthly repayments are going to be,' said Wanless. 'But Free-if-in-Credit is an expensive system. It was forced upon us, so we have to make our money out of other services. We do not have the luxury of offering a cost-plus service. But once people have a current account and confidence in the bank then we can on-sell. Free-if-in-Credit would have been much more difficult if we had not had mortgages to make money on. In that sense we have got a lot to learn from retailers about packaging services and building relationships with customers.'

It is hard to build a relationship through a bullet-proof screen, so NatWest and the other banks have pulled in the design consultants to come up with a softer look based on carpets, curtains and chats across a desk. The key to this is the timelock till, which can be programmed to release only so much cash each time it is opened. Most personal customers do not ask for more than £200 per visit. The old-style 'fortress' counter can be tucked away in the corner to cope with richer individuals and business customers.

'We see ourselves spurred on by competition and improved technology,' Wanless explained. 'We have had 3,000 factories on the high street, which will now become more general retail outlets. Our branch staff are moving from work processing to selling as technology enables us to shift the work processing to centres away from the high street. So we are playing around with branch design. It's a question of how we can best make use of the space. There has been much more pressure on the branches, because the network has not increased while the volume of business has. But the Automated Teller Machines have done a lot to relieve that pressure. And we have started to change the way we look at the network, for example by developing 100 corporate business centres round the country. We are learning from other retailers.'

And not before time. The department stores have noted the success of Sears Roebuck in the US at selling insurance, stocks and shares and other financial services. Marks & Spencer has been granted a deposit-taking licence, to the undisguised dread of British banks. Debenhams already has share shops in addition to its highly profitable Welbeck Finance. If someone needs a loan to buy a lounge suite, why let them go off to a bank for the money when you can provide it yourself and take a second slice of profit?

And it is largely one-way competition. Although there is some scope for the banks to sell goods through credit card mailing shots, the fact is that is is much easier for a store to set up a financial desk than it is for NatWest to sell shirts and socks. People are in a mood to be sold a loan to pay for goods they have just agreed to buy, but they are not usually in a mood to be sold goods when they have just negotiated a loan. Wanless admitted: 'Other retailers are a threat. They are in the enviable position of deciding what they want to do and picking off what they want.'

Until recently banks have been dominated by systems and internal procedures which dictated the primacy of lending to companies, for that was where the significant profits were to be made. That is still true, but the personal customer is a profitable prospect too, and the banks realise that they are going to have to fight to retain their share of that market. So the big change in thinking has been to put the customer first.

'We used to assume we knew what our customers wanted,' said Wanless. 'Now we are getting used to asking them, and trying things out. We have Home Buyers' Kits, for first and second time buyers. We have a New Account Pack, because it is vitally important to make the right initial impression. We used to assume people knew what they wanted when they opened an account. Then we did some research and found some surprising things out, like they don't necessarily know what is available.'

Saturday banking demonstrates the shift in attitudes. When the banks closed their doors on Saturdays in 1969 the building societies picked up plenty of business simply by staying open on a day when people wanted to use them. After Barclays reopened on Saturdays in August 1982 the others duly followed and they have begun to exploit the opportunity to woo back the lost custom. Until 1969 Saturday was a normal banking day, offering the complete range of services. Now it is devoted to personal business. There is machinery to get cash in and out, together with desks for chatting to customers, solving problems by selling them extra services.

'We come back to customer needs,' said Wanless. 'They want cash, a safe place to leave their money, a convenient place to borrow, insurance, mortgages, maybe stocks and shares. Product design is very important. We have the Access Gold Plus, which offers a direct line into our stockbroker, County Securities, the ability to withdraw more cash through the Access system, free banking, a direct debiting facility and a £10,000 borrowing facility. It also takes away a lot of the need to use a branch, which cuts down queues. The good products are the ones that are thought through and much more related to the market, and more convenient for the customer.'

The challenge confronting the banks is to differentiate themselves from one another, as the rest of the high street is doing. But that is easier said than done, after decades in which they have all been content to present the same image of respectability and trustworthiness. The older branches look like miniature versions

159

of the Bank of England, complete with granite pillars and windows too high to let anyone see in. That is now out of date, but they have still to discover what it is that generates a particular image of an attractive and friendly bank in the public's mind.

NatWest has discovered to its dismay that many people perceive a greater difference between branches of the same bank than they do between banks. This means that NatWest and the others have not achieved that uniformity of public response that mainstream retailers often manage to achieve, and that worries them. It suggests that standards of service and friendliness vary from branch to branch, a discrepancy that can be removed only by better staff training. Yet overlaying these impressions is a feeling that one bank is very much like another, despite their huge advertising campaigns. It amounts to the worst of both worlds.

National Westminster is one of the biggest life insurance brokers, which gives the bank a direct link in to mortgages through advice on endowment policies, pensions and so on. 'Again that is a question of training staff,' Wanless pointed out, 'but they are very receptive to change because they welcome the customer contact, and to do that they have to feel confident that they can answer the questions. We have Home Loans Officers, and there is much more specialisation of staff within the branches.'

That process will be extended if NatWest is to make a go of selling stocks and shares through its branches, now that it owns a stockbroker. The plan is for customers to use machines to buy and sell securities, with staff there to help them. They are putting Prestel sets into some branches, to give instant share quotations, and video screens which would-be investors can press to get the answer to a particular question. But only when customer preferences have become clearer can NatWest decide if they should provide simply a dealing service using technology, or whether more advice is needed.

'Much depends on the spread of wider share ownership,' Wanless explained. 'We are creating an image of a place where people can go to deal in securities, and at the same time finding out for ourselves.' A bear market, with share prices falling, will be the test for securities trading. So far it's been a one-way bet, and it has been largely based on privatisations like British Telecom and British Gas as well as the Trustee Savings Bank. They have found it easy to attract new investors because they only had to fill in an application form. But trading in existing securities involves help and advice.'

In-house share shops are just one of a range of potential new 'products' that NatWest and the other high street banks will have to make decisions about in the next few years. More than ever before those products will be driven by consumer choice and the threat or reality of competing alternatives offered by building societies, specialist financial service retailers and non-financial chains increasingly anxious to sell everything complementary to their shop-window goods – including the money to pay for them.

THE HALIFAX PRODUCES A LITTLE XTRA

The Old Cock Inn is an unlikely-sounding birthplace for a £30 billion organisation serving a quarter of the adult population of this country. But that was the name of the pub used by a group of Yorkshiremen in 1852 who wanted to form what was then known as a permanent benefit building and investment society. The following February the Halifax Permanent Benefit Building Society was founded. Since 1913 it has been the biggest of its kind in Britain, and is now as big as any comparable organisation in the world.

No other country has anything quite like the British building society, although a number have institutions whose aim is to attract and provide finance for home buying, like America's Savings and Loan Associations. The original idea was dreamed up in Birmingham in 1775 by craftsmen who could not afford to build houses for themselves. So they each put part of their wages into a pool to buy materials and built the houses in their spare time. They drew lots to decide who should have each house as it was completed. When everyone had a home the project wound itself up.

These early ventures were known as terminating societies. But it did not take long to develop the principle of a permanent building society, acting purely as a middle-man between savers and people who wanted to borrow to buy a house. They were and are non-profit making, and are owned by depositors. Although well-run societies do prudently amass surpluses, that money still technically belongs to depositors and the management takes only enough to cover salaries and expenses. The ethos of mutual self-help has given them an unparalleled status and even affection in the eyes of the public.

For a long time that ethos discouraged the building societies from exploiting their customers or even selling at them too hard. This meant that until recently they were perhaps slower to compete for the saver's pound and take advantage of the opportunities presented by the new technology. 'As a general marketing concept, it's quite surprising that ten years ago we only had two products, and we didn't call them products,' said Jim Birrell, the Halifax's Operations Director. 'All our mortgages were at one rate of interest and we had only one type of paid-up share account.'

Not any more. The most noticeable marketing change by the societies has been to present their financial services in different packages for different markets. In common with other building societies, the Halifax has home start and endowment mortgages and a proliferation of fixed-term shares and those with differing notice periods. A short-term money-management account is in the pipeline.

The Halifax also has Cardcash, arguably the most sophisticated of the through-the-wall machine networks. Apart from the standard cash deposits and withdrawals, and instant statements, Cardcash also allows customers to shift money from one account to another, and pay bills. You key in the account number of whoever you want to pay, such as the electricity board, and the amount, and the money is automatically transferred. In one week not so long ago no less than 25 per cent of Halifax customers' transactions went through its 450 Cardcash machines.

And with a display of the sort of grit that many a fellow Yorkshireman will surely applaud, the Halifax has been remarkably hard-nosed about its creation. Said Birrell: 'We have gone it alone as a building society on Automated Teller Machines, which is what the Cardcash machines are. We are not part of the Link or Matrix consortia which other building societies belong to.

NatWest chases the teenage and children's markets.

Halifax customers queue to use the Cardcash machine.

It may sound hard, but we are in advance of the field technically, so it would have helped our competitors more than us to have gone into a consortium. We think our system is richer, and our technical edge stops the banks from doing a 'me-too'. While sharing seems attractive, it's not so beneficial in a relatively small island like the UK. We looked at going in with the Giro Bank, but when we studied it we discovered that almost all of their machines would have been within 400 yards of ours, so there was little to be gained. It makes more sense internationally, or if we could link with a Scottish bank, because they have better representation in Scotland.'

The ever-unpredictable relationship between man and machine has taught the Halifax one or two intriguing lessons about human nature. Until they introduced Cardcash in 1978 the management did not realise how embarrassed people felt about asking for their own money, and how easily they could be put off or offended. Before hole-in-the-wall machines, customers had no option but to swallow their discomfort. Now they have an escape.

'We found that people don't tend to use ATMs as they said they would,' Birrell said. 'When we asked them what they would want an ATM for, they said for getting money outside office hours, or when they were away from home. But most use it at their home branch during office hours.'

The Halifax started using computers later than other banks and building societies. In the late 70s they jumped straight from written ledgers to an IBM system for the savings and mortgage accounts. By then the banks had been wired up for years – but only after some expensive teething troubles. The Halifax skipped that stage, learned from others' mistakes and gained a clearer idea of the potential to be squeezed out of computers. Its system is fully integrated, so new ideas cannot simply be plugged in. That makes it less flexible, but more powerful.

As the banks have found, the computer frees the staff to spend more time with customers. As the society has expanded its branch network to more than 700 it has introduced the concept of much warmer and friendlier offices, though security measures have had to be taken into consideration when designing the new offices.

The compromise, also adopted by the banks, has been to design open-plan branches with desks for interviews, but with the bulk of the cash in a secure corner of the room. Another recent innovation has been the concept of a local office that does not offer a full service because it is linked to the headquarters by a computer.

But computers have also threatened the long-standing idea of the agency office, under which solicitors and the like handle Halifax business. It was a cheap way of extending the branch network, but in the era of on-line technology the society is having to decide whether to supply an agency with a computer, in which case it becomes more like a mini-branch, or drop it from the list altogether.

This in turn must increase the traffic going through the branches, offset only by higher use of Cardcash. 'We have had a very heavy pressure on the branches,' Birrell admitted. That pressure was stepped up after 1969, when the banks were rash enough to close on Saturdays, a decision they reversed thirteen years later.

'The banks closing on Saturdays gave us a great psychological edge,' said Birrell. 'Banks were seen as an organisation to suit the bank clerk, rather than the customer, which meant that many more people came through our doors after 1969. We were the first to introduce centralised queuing in a major way. People like to keep moving when they are in a queue. They are more likely to do that in a single queue, and it focuses management's attention on the customer if they can see one line of people in the centre of the room.'

Those lines are now being cut by the growing use of Cardcash, and an increasing use of direct mail, using its customer base to sell related services by post.

Related, or additional, services promise to figure more prominently in the building society of the future, thanks to the 1986 Building Society Act, which came into force in January 1987. That Act gives the bigger societies the right to lend more freely and to go into new areas such as estate agencies and even stockbroking.

The Halifax has taken advantage of the new law to go into unsecured lending, until now primarily the preserve of the banks and the source of much of their bread-and-butter dealings with the personal customer. Before this year the societies were restricted to lending against the security of their customers' houses through the mortgage mechanism. If someone wanted to borrow to build an extension, then a second mortgage could be raised, assuming there was enough of a margin between the first mortgage and the current value of the property. If not, the societies had to reject the application.

In recent years a growing proportion of these second mortgages have been used to buy things unconnected with the house, like a car or even a holiday. Strictly speaking it was against the rules to do that, but in today's more competitive atmosphere some societies turned a blind eye to the practice. Now the blinkers have been removed. 'Our unsecured lending will principally be in connection with things for the home, kitchen equipment and furniture,' said Birrell, 'but we are considering offering an overdraft facility on Cardcash.'

In September 1986 the Nationwide became the first building society to join the race to develop an estate agency chain, a race led until then by Lloyds Bank and Prudential Assurance. Two weeks later the Halifax entered the running, aiming to take over 200 such offices by the end of 1987. It seems a natural extension for a building society's activities, but Birrell has his reservations.

'The problem with estate agents is that people do quarrel with them, and that worries us,' he pointed out. 'Either they blame the agent for recommending too high a price, so its takes a long time to sell the house, or it goes quickly and they blame the agent for talking them into too low a price.' That could have unforeseen consequences for the building societies' carefully preserved caring image. It will need delicate handling.

Hitherto the only unpopular action a society has had to take has been to repossess a house if the owner could not keep up the mortgage repayments, and then usually with large helpings of sympathy and understanding. It will be a trickier matter if, say, the Halifax has also sold the house to the luckless occupant in its role as an estate agent.

That is one reason why the Halifax is hesitating about offering a facility for buying and selling stocks and shares. 'We have a dilemma,' Birrell said. 'With our market reputation, we do not want to recommend people to go into risk investment because the Halifax recommends they do it. If it went wrong, our reputation would suffer. But if the customer wants the service, we may do it. The Trustee Savings Bank and British Gas share flotations showed how people have acquired a taste for riskier investment. Personal pensions are a different matter. It's a high security investment, and it involves us in high identification. People like to know what is happening to their money. There is a clear niche there for us.'

The Halifax feels on safer ground moving into insurance policies as a broker. It already sells life assurance and buildings insurance as an agent, and will soon offer redundancy and accident policies. Motor insurance may follow. The society has a preferred list of insurance companies that it advises its branch managers to use, and they can call the latest rates and performance on a Viewdata screen.

Doubtless many of the Halifax's ten million customers will rush to embrace these new services. But in the process the very nature of the Halifax and its closest building society rivals may irreversibly change. They and the banks are becoming more like one another all the time, and the societies' fear is that they will lose their special appeal to the public in the midst of the melée to sell every type of financial service from every street corner. By then some of the high ideals hammered out at the Old Cock Inn more than a century ago may be lost for ever.

The
Eating, Drinking and
Make-believe Show

THE PROTAGONISTS:
- McDONALD'S
- ALLIED LYONS

The food trade in Britain is in many ways a thankless one, but not without its excitement for those of a cannibalistic disposition. As there are very few undernourished people in Britain, it is difficult for the food and drink business to grow much faster than the population, which means that the companies involved have to take sales off one another if they are to expand. The supermarkets have been coming to grips with this problem for some years, by taking business off the corner shops and tempting customers with a steady flow of new foods and made-up dishes which add value, businessman's jargon for raising profit margins. Now the gap between the pub and snack bar at one end of the spectrum and the fully-blown restaurant at the other end is being filled by a rush of new retail catering ventures with very much the same idea in mind.

Just as a ready-prepared supermarket dish like tandoori chicken gives that taste of the exotic for a slightly higher price, so a hamburger and milk shake can give a momentary flavour of the United States and an imitation French brasserie can transport its customers across the Channel for an evening. And every extra meal that people eat out eats into the supermarkets' turnover. The battle to fill the public's stomach is becoming increasingly fierce and wide ranging.

To the extent that the high street revolution is a lifestyle revolution, it is bound to affect the catering trade. If the young and fashionable are going to be persuaded to mould their wardrobes around the collections of Next or Top Shop, they are going to want to show off those clothes in a suitable setting, yet one which they can afford. And as clothes become a more inventive means of self-expression, so the social environments also have to become more innovative and individualistic. A good pub or restaurant gradually fits round its regulars like a coat.

The message of the moment is flexibility. That means that the caterers have to be more willing to change, update, redecorate, give the customer what he or she wants. Britain, beginning with the better-travelled communities of London and the south-east and spreading outwards, is converting to the American notion of letting the customers eat or drink as much or as little as they feel like, within the limitations of the licensing laws. This is indeed a revolution, in a country which has prided itself in the past on catering for the caterer's convenience rather than the customer's.

One of the longest-lasting catering franchises is Wimpy, which by the mid-1970s had become rundown and tatty, serving greasy hamburgers to a public which knew no better. That came under challenge from the Kaye brothers, who have a knack of inventing reasonably-priced restaurants in the London area. They developed Golden Egg and now run Garfunkels Restaurants, which also owns Deep Pan Pizza. The pizza has been running the hamburger a close second as the universal cheap but-exotic meal through chains like Pizzaland and Pizza Hut, the latter a Pepsi-Cola franchise operated in Britain by Whitbread, the brewers.

Suddenly choice was opening out. The easy target was still the hamburger, which some caterers realised could be made into a more expensive novelty than Wimpy had conceived, by using better materials, making the product bigger and serving it in more comfortable surroundings. One of those who latched onto the possibilities was Michael Golder, a polytechnic lecturer who bought Brookes Restaurant in Knightsbridge in 1973. 'The code word then was "American",' said Golder. 'If you described your hamburgers as American that meant "not Wimpy",' he recalled.

Only a year later the UK hamburger market was never to be the same again. McDonald's opened its 3,000th branch and first in Britain, in Woolwich. It was slow to expand, but the writing was on the wall for the competition. United Biscuits bought the Wimpy franchise in 1978 and soon began upgrading it into a McDonald's lookalike. Out went waitress service. In came the US formula of queuing for what you wanted and either taking it to your table or taking it out into the street.

Other competitors decided to get out of McDonald's way. 'It's one thing to take on a lumbering giant,' said Golder, 'but it's quite another matter to take on a lean, efficient giant who is determined to expand. After McDonald's, there was no way we could be the market leader in that part of the business.' He either sold his hamburger outlets, or converted them into restaurants with other themes in his Kennedy Brookes chain.

Wine bars revived in the 1970s, initially as a way for Luis Gordon, a wine shipper, to sell its wines more actively. But they caught a mood. They offered something different, wine had become relatively cheap, and there was a latent demand from women for somewhere fashionable to drink that was more congenial than a pub. The brewers should have been in the best position to take advantage of the new trend, but they were predictably slow to tumble what was going on, possibly because they had been distracted by the Campaign for Real Ale, which attacked mass-produced keg beer.

So it was some time before most pubs would sell wine by the bottle, or spend money on redecorating to attract the new audience. What they did not realise was the way in which the new drinking and eating public was willing to be seduced by street theatre. This was something that the flamboyant, bow-tied Golder saw very early on, and he is now the impresario of Wheeler's, Mario and Franco and the Café des Amis du Vin. He explained: 'It's like a live performance every night, and to make that work as a business you have got to make it as reliable as possible. It can be remarkably difficult. Either a dish will be popular for a few weeks and then suddenly die, or a really good one will be too hard for the chefs to be sure of getting right every time. After all, it may be just one mistake on the night for him, but for the customer it could be a special anniversary dinner spoiled.'

This puts an additional pressure on the new breed of caterers to perform. McDonald's has shown what can be done with a strictly trained staff operating a superbly streamlined system, but as their management would be the first to admit, they achieve that by keeping the menu simple and, in particular, avoiding alcohol. there are compensations from serving liquor, not least because the customer's own judgment becomes a little wayward as the meal progresses, but it does make the control task more complicated.

The popular answer has been to import the American coffee-house system, backed by computerised stock monitoring and a microwave oven. While these places can be dressed in an infinite number of ways, they work on the common principle that the customer can order anything, anytime.

Whitbread started the Pizza Hut franchise because they anticipated the change in the licensing laws and wanted to explore what that could mean in terms of flexible hours. Lots of people have got in on the pizza idea, but meanwhile Whitbread is able to sell pizzas in its pubs and experiment with drinks in Pizza Hut. It has also taken out another US franchise, T.G.I. Friday. (In case you are wondering, T.G.I. stands for 'Thank God It's'.)

That is what much of the eating-out market is about these days, a joke a minute and any credit card will do. But it is at least enlivening the high street and looks set to keep doing so. The breathalyser has seen to that. Rural pub trade is down, and in any case the out-of-town restaurant business was always a specialised one, relying on secluded sites. It is difficult to cash in on economies of scale by building bigger and bigger restaurants. People simply do not want to feel they are eating in a barn, so big eateries have to be cleverly designed. The new shopping centres tend to close too early for the caterers, who therefore prefer to take space on the outer edge of such developments, so that they can stay open after the shops have closed. If the shops could be persuaded to stay open, we could be faced with a new type of café society.

BIG MAC MOVES IN

Whenever anyone is tempted to write off the high street, they should just stop and think of McDonald's. It is fashionable to deride this US-based hamburger chain as selling junk food to an uncritical mass market, and the group has put considerable effort into getting across the nutritional value of its products in the face of such criticism. But after a slow and cautious start in this country it has 250 outlets and is aiming to be in every sizeable high street with a chain of around 1,000 by the end of the century.

McDonald's depends on passing trade every bit as much as any of its rivals in the light meal business. But many customers drive cars to the high street locations, causing congestion at peak times. A large proportion of those journeys are to collect meals that are either eaten in the car or taken home. So at the end of 1986 the firm opened its first British drive-through branches, surrounded by a car park but with a separate counter to serve drivers in their vehicles. That will take McDonald's beyond the high street and into competition with roadside chains such as Little Chef and Happy Eater.

McDonald's is above all dominated by systems that are repeatable all over the world. Although there is some room to experiment with different designs – the Bromley branch in Kent is a picturesque example – each branch conforms to a set pattern. You go through the entrance, past the seating area to the counter at the back. All the spare space is used for tables, so that the restaurant always seems crowded even when it is empty. The menu, which is well-nigh identical everywhere, is displayed high up behind the counter so that customers can choose while they are queuing to be served. The hot food is made up in batches which have to be timed to meet the ups and downs in demand throughout the day, because if it is left lying for more than eleven minutes it is thrown away. Drinks are on tap. All the containers are disposable and there are no knives or forks.

McDonald's has taken the supermarket principles of simplicity, convenience and cleanliness and translated them into a strictly limited, strictly controlled equivalent of a café. But it is not a café. Until the first UK branch opened in Woolwich, south London, in 1974 virtually the only self-service eating was in sandwich bars. There, in the reverse of McDonald's layout, the counter is normally at the front of the shop and the tables at the back. Fish and chip shops were almost entirely devoted to the takeaway trade. Otherwise, if you wanted to sit you had to have your order taken and food brought to your table by a waiter or waitress.

'The US has led the way in eating out,' Michael Hayden, the UK marketing vice-president, explained. 'It has the disposable income and wants convenience, and the two have gone hand in hand elsewhere as standards have risen. McDonald's has helped to open up and expand what convenience is about. Aspirations are rising, more people travel abroad, so they know what standards of service can be provided. And McDonald's has a formula that is acceptable. We work very hard at keeping things simple.'

To achieve that, their restaurants have to get a high volume of business. They cost more than £750,000 each to build and equip, without taking account of property prices, so they have to work hard to pay their way. McDonald's keeps its financial figures close to its chest, but with those overheads annual sales have to get up to around £1 million per branch for the operation to make better sense than putting the money in a bank deposit account. That works out at an average of £2,500 a day all year round, and with an average spend of something like £2.50 per head per visit, a thousand people have to push their way through the doors of each branch each day for the sums to add up.

That is no mean feat, and shows why those hamburgers have to come up the same time after time after time. If the 250 branches each have to attract about 360,000 customers a year, that comes to ninety million visits, which is one and a half times the population of the UK. Allow for the fact that McDonald's does not yet have saturation coverage and it is easy to see that the group has to be reliable enough to make people come back again and again.

The pressure on reliability is reinforced by the fact that McDonald's main appeal is to children, with or without parents. That is why its advertising is carefully targeted at two audiences: the Ronald McDonald clown and his friends for the children, and a bright and breezy approach for the under-40s who are likely to have young families.

The idea behind McDonald's took root in 1954, when Ray Kroc, a maker of milk shake machines, went to see what was then the one and only branch of McDonald's in San Bernardino, California. He went because the two McDonald brothers who ran it had bought eight of his machines. Most restaurants bought only one. He sat in his car and watched streams of people driving up and queuing for hamburgers, fries and, of course, milk shakes. He sampled the food and spent two days watching.

If Kroc could persuade the brothers to open more branches he could sell more milk shake machines. But they did not want to, so he bought a licence to operate McDonald's branches himself. It snowballed. In 1961 Kroc bought out the McDonald brothers for £1 million. Now there are more than 9,000 stores, as the company calls them, and McDonald's claims to be the biggest fast-service restaurant chain in the world. 'We take the business of making hamburgers more seriously than anyone else,' they say, and it is easy to believe them. When McDonald's went nationwide across the US with Chicken McNuggets in 1983, after four years' test marketing, it immediately became the world's second largest user of chicken.

For an operation on that scale to produce reliable meals that customers can trust, it must itself have supplies it can rely on and a staff which can be trusted to process those raw materials from lorry to counter. It is to Britain's shame that this is the only country in which McDonald's has had to set up its own companies to make buns and hamburgers the way it wants them, in the quantities and consistency it wants. 'It would be fair to say that UK suppliers in the mid-70s were not up to the standards we wanted,' said Hayden, who is himself British. 'Especially, they could not keep the consistency, which was vital to us. In Britain we are atypical in doing that. Certainly it doesn't happen in America, and I can't think of any other country where we have set up our own lines of supply'.

So McKey Foods operates the most advanced meat plant in Europe at Milton Keynes, and Golden West Foods bakes buns at Hemel Hempstead and distributes the group's supplies to the stores. They are each owned jointly by McDonald's and their managing directors.

Many people deride McDonald's staff training as so much brainwashing, largely because of its insistence on calling the training centres Hamburger Universities, and referring to its diplomas as Bachelor of Hamburgerology degrees. While that smacks of American brashness that jars on British ears, it belies an approach to selection and training that compares with any other retailer, Marks & Spencer included.

Intending employees have an introductory interview, two days' on-the-job experience and a second interview based on reports that the candidate and his branch manager write after the two days' work. Says the company: 'At any of these stages the process can be halted, either by us or by you, with no hard feelings. Afterwards, we both finally decide whether we're right for each other.'

Everyone, even if recruited for a management job, starts by spending at least a few months in uniform working in a branch and learning from practical experience how important timing is. Then they can climb the ladder, learning floor control, people management, accounting procedures, the psychology of motivation and advanced leadership skills. Yes, it does sound a little elaborate for a hamburger joint, but by taking themselves seriously McDonald's encourages others to do likewise.

'The principles are quite simple,' Hayden explained. 'Work hard at it, take care of people. There is a lot of hype in the store. If you get personnel hyping the store, combined with teamwork, then it is successful. What we want is the ability to work in a team and to lead it. But it is important to show we care. We have rap sessions every month or so to let people have their moans and groans about how things are working. I did four weeks in a store when I joined. I thought it was a bit over the top at first, but it was worth it. I wanted a flavour across the board: a West End store, a suburban store, opening in the morning, late nights. I suppose the job I liked least was unloading product from the trucks. But I enjoyed being on the grill.'

Everyone in what is known as the crew circulates from the front of the store to the counter, the grill area, back-up stores – and unloading. It teaches future executives little things like not to phone a store between 12.30 and two o'clock unless they have to, because that is when it is really busy. If someone is particularly good at one job, then the manager has the discretion to make sure the person spends more than the usual amount of time doing that. Most crew members are under 21 and in their first job, and so are more malleable than more experienced workers. They are paid hourly and work shifts within the fifteen hours a day a store is normally open.

Given the greater affluence of those who have a job in Britain, and the more relaxed attitudes to eating out, McDonald's should be finding itself coming up against competition on every street corner. But although many other firms have tried it, competing with McDonald's has proved to be little fun. It has no monopoly on what it does and provides, but more than one would-be rival has decided that there are better ways of earning a living than fighting the goliath of the industry. Others who were already in catering and now find themselves wrestling with McDonald's every working day would dearly like to sell out and try something more peaceful. But there is no queue of buyers for a business which can never be more than a distant number two.

The more successful McDonald's is the bigger it becomes, for new branches are built out of the cash flow from the existing stores. Like Marks & Spencer, it does not go in for taking over rivals, preferring to grow its own culture from the roots. After four years in Britain it had only nine stores. In the past nine years it has opened another 240, and the pace is still accelerating.

Although McDonald's is gradually expanding its menu, it will only ever claim a part of the eating-out market. What Ray Kroc did, once he had got his hands on the licence, was to identify a segment of the market and serve it better than anyone else, using the chain principle to give him bulk-buying power and to reassure the public that they would get the same product in every branch – whether they are in Tokyo or Tooting. 'Catering is a target involving eating, which is always emotional,' said Hayden. 'It's important to take that element of uncertainty out of it.'

PUBS, BRASSERIES AND COUNTRY CLUBS

Once upon a time, the pubs opened their doors and waited for the customers to roll in. They had the field to themselves in terms of offering people an easy and cheap escape from dingy homes, and they perfectly fitted the prevailing view that the standard night out consisted of men drinking beer with other men, while their women stayed at home.

Higher living standards, foreign holidays and assertion of women's rights have put paid to that, at least in the south of England. the pubs have had to react accordingly. Not that there was ever just the one sort of pub, thanks to regional and historical variations. But now those variations are being played up as part of deliberate marketing tactics. Whether or not they feature music, pubs are part of entertainment, and they face much stronger competiton than before for their share of people's leisure spending – a large slice of which is devoted by many to their homes and the amusement equipment they can now contain.

Malcolm Wright, corporate director of Allied Breweries, the Ansells, Ind Coope and Tetleys pub group which also owns the Victoria Wine off-licence chain, said: 'The take-home trade has made a difference, and we take the point about pubs becoming relatively less attractive than people's homes. At one time people went to the pub to get away from their homes. The only answer is to keep the pub looking better than people's homes. We are upgrading them so that they offer more food and activities, so that we can charge a higher margin. There is a lot of scope for changing people's lifestyles, through the conversion to the American tendency to eat out. London is leading in that.'

Nowadays Allied, part of the giant Allied-Lyons food and drinks group, tries to target its outlets, and differentiate between different outlets in the same area. It does that by local research, finding out what people want, seeing what is being provided and what the competition is offering. 'We try and segment them,' Wright explained, 'but not necessarily to appeal to just one section of the community. The classic appeal to one segment is the disco pub, which aims at 18-25 year-olds looking for a partner, and who want a noisy atmosphere. Otherwise, most of our pubs appeal to different sections, and often at different times of the day. It may be a businessman's pub at lunchtime and a local in the evening.'

One of the thorns in the side of the big pub chains over the past two decades has been the Campaign for Real Ale, which criticised the volume brewers for abandoning cask-conditioned 'real' ale in favour of the more manageable but gassier keg beer. CAMRA was for years dismissed as an eccentric if trendy sideshow, but in its 1986 annual report Allied-Lyons proudly announced that it had won two of the three CAMRA awards for pub preservation. More to the point, the shrewder brewers have jumped on the real ale bandwagon as a good excuse to put up their prices. London beer drinkers have to reach into their pockets for a £1 coin and more wherever they see a traditional beer pump on the bar counter. For in today's climate a 'real ale' pub is just another retail product, depending on the drinker's mood and taste.

Though most tipplers do not like to admit it, choice of beer is a low-priority reason for going to a particular pub. Above that come meeting friends, the atmosphere of the pub, the landlord, and how near it is. On average people travel two miles to their regular pub, according to Wright, but it can vary enormously depending on whether it is in the town or the country.

'We make a distinction between local pubs and destination pubs,' said Wright. 'Locals have to respond to traditional demands and changes in the ethnic mix. Destination pubs are more for food or entertainment like a disco, and we can often ask people to pay more for what they perceive as higher value.'

In what has become a large-scale version of the publican's traditional desire to be all things to all men, Allied has joined the

177

other brewers in producing a range of eating and drinking venues. New ones are coming out all the time, enabling Allied to ring the changes more quickly and flexibly than before.

'The consumer is looking for more than a traditional boozer,' said Wright. 'There are now few places where food of some sort is not served. More people are looking to eat out. People are becoming more adventurous, so everyone in the business has to be more adventurous to attract them. To that end we have evolved a series of different catering outlets.'

A showpiece is Calendars in Watford, a 240-seat US-style café/bar/restaurant, with plenty of car parking. There is a central bar with eating facilities all around it. Calendars serves 3,500 meals a week on the basis of a menu ranging from enchilada to Sunday roast. Richard Martin, the chairman and chief executive of Allied Breweries, describes the venture as 'immensely successful' and plans to open 25 Calendars by 1991.

Other chains include Cavaliers and Diners in the north, Golden Oak Inns and Country Inns in the midlands and Chesters, Exchanges and Muswells in the south. Most offer American-style eating, in the sense of informal, please-yourself menus, with international beers, and they are open all day, although they have to conform to the licensing laws by not selling alcohol out of hours.

Allied has been careful not to forget steak bars, which still do very well because most people are still basically conservative despite the trend towards lighter food, so that is the market that Chesters and Cavaliers cater for.

London is still the testbed for new ideas and ideas that will not work anywhere else. The Soho Brasserie is an example of a themed outlet that Allied may repeat in London, but is unlikely to try elsewhere. It captures the continental feel convincingly enough to have been given *The Times* Brasserie of the Year award, and appeals to a huge mix of people. It succeeds as a piece of street theatre, and that is where the demand lies in high street catering.

That has been pushed – so far – to its limit in Gamebirds, a chain of Allied pubs going under names like the Bitter End, Cock 'n' Bull and the Last Straw, in Watford, Corby, Romford, Cobham and Derby. As the jolly titles suggest, the pubs are aimed at young people, and Allied asked a young designer called Sassoon to do them up. He has largely filled them with junk like old sewing machines, and in one outlet an entire wall is covered with old

Killing time in Gateshead Metro Centre.

HOT HOT..HOT...HOT...

on the heels of the
fashion challenge...

JEFFREY
ROGERS

1
SWEATER
£17.99
SIZES 10-16
2 COLOURS

1

2

3

1 **SWEATER**
LOOSE FITTING STYLE WITH
CREW NECK COLLAR.
ACRYLIC, WASHABLE.
SIZES: 10/12; 14/16.
BS 3672 NAVY
BS 3673 GREEN
£17.99 20 wks 90p

4

5

6

6

For Plimsolls please
see page 317

2
SKIRT
£11.99
SIZES 10-16
2 COLOURS

we come up with
all the
Answers

2

3
DRESS
£24.99
SIZES 10-16
2 COLOURS

For belt
see pages 46/7

be streets ahead in
stripes, navy or green
. . . the perfect match
for work or play.

5
CARDIGAN
£21.99
SIZES 10-16
2 COLOURS

6
SKIRT
£13.99
SIZES 10-16
2 COLOURS

4
SHIRT
£21.99
SIZES 10-16
2 COLOURS

2   MINI SKIRT
IN BOLD STRIPES. ACRYLIC.
LENGTH 18 INS. WASHABLE.
SIZES: 10/12; 14/16.
BS 1470   NAVY
BS 1471   GREEN
£21.99 20 wks 60p

3   DRESS
HAS WHITE COLLAR AND
PLACKET. COTTON JERSEY.
WASHABLE. LENGTH 43 INS.
SIZES: 10/12; 14/16.
BS 4419   NAVY
BS 4420   GREEN
£24.99 20 wks £1.25

4   RUGBY SHIRT
TRADITIONALLY STRIPED
FOR IMPACT. COTTON
JERSEY. WASHABLE.
SIZES: 10/12; 14/16.
BS 7163   NAVY
BS 7164   GREEN
£21.99 20 wks £1.10

5   CARDIGAN
EASY FITTING IN COTTON
JERSEY. WASHABLE.
SIZES: 10/12; 14/16.
BS 3634   NAVY
BS 3635   GREEN
£21.99 20 wks £1.10

6   TUBE SKIRT
WITH BUTTON BACK HEM.
COTTON JERSEY. WASHABLE.
LENGTH 31 INS.
SIZES: 10/12; 14/16.
BS 1432   NAVY
BS 1433   GREEN
£13.99 20 wks 70p

6

3

Seventies severity at Brent Cross, north London.

Babycham crates. The late Sir Keith Showering would probably approve. He was the former chairman of Allied whose family invented Babycham, one of the most profitable drinks ever marketed.

Out of town, Allied's Embassy Hotels chain owns the Gloucester Hotel and Country Club, which has golf, squash, tennis, table tennis, a dry ski slope and a jacuzzi. In Milton Keynes the group has a pub by a lake that offers boating, pitch & putt, tennis and table tennis.

In the midst of all this commercial slapstick and greasepaint, it very nearly comes as a surprise to learn that the traditional pub has also been able to turn its hand to all-purpose restaurants in the managed outlets, while tenants operate their own packages. The whole pub grub business has been transformed by the microwave oven, the foundation of more than one catering fortune in the past few years.

'Brewers are producing many more professional retailing ideas,' said Wright, 'and the controls have to come from inside, which argues in favour of using the managed houses. They give us much more scope for control. The tenant is a business in his own right, although we can vary how long a lease he has, and indeed how many tenancies we allow him. A large number have multiple tenancies.'

The character of the pub is changing as restrictions are gradually taken off, for children and in other ways. The Calendars-type places are blurring the lines betwen bars and restuarants. It has long been possible for children to have a meal at the same table as adults who are consuming alcohol, but until not so long ago children were not allowed in a bar area where drinking alcohol was the whole object. In many parts of the country the authorities are becoming more relaxed about this question, so the brewers and other caterers can be more creative about new projects.

But there are still wide regional variations, depending on the attitude of the local council or police chief. And one thing the brewers do not want to do is to provoke the simmering anti-alcohol lobby. They have seen what such tactics have done to the tobacco industry, and they do not want to suffer a similar fate.

Said Wright: 'We cannot advertise drinks in cinemas, and we have been nervous of doing too much sponsorship of sport or the arts in case it gives us too high a profile and provokes the anti-alcohol lobby and possibly risks legislation, as happened with the tobacco companies. Unlike them, though, we believe that there is a lot of support for the role of the public house as a social centre. In that it is unique in the world.'

Allied is fortunate in having such a large estate of tied public houses at a time of such flux in high street catering. This gives it an opportunity to experiment with people and premises in a way that is denied to lesser organisations, and to capitalise on successful formulae. Like other retailers, the cashdesk computer has dramatically altered the economics of these new ventures, by cutting pilferage and improving stock controls, as well as giving a constant stream of market research data.

Unlike McDonald's the Allied outlets attempt to offer the setting for meals that normally demand some sense of occasion, from a Sunday lunch to a birthday treat. The growth of this form of eating out will rely on whether Allied and its competitors can capture the mood, and whether they can persuade more people to think in terms of going out for a meal. To that extent they are competing with television, the very different eating experience being sold by the supermarkets – and the comfort of people's own homes.

Streetwise to the End

Undeniably, the retail revolution has been great fun, almost a spectator sport. Design has become the buzz-word of the high street. The design consultancies have made fortunes out of helping to launch new 'themed' chains, which has led to commissions to smarten the dowdier retail chains, kidding the public that those shops are more in tune with the times than they were before yesterday's lick of paint. Retailing has become more flexible and responsive, and underlying these shifts has been a tougher attitude to selling. A once staid, even stodgy business has turned into a game of leapfrog. One idea after another has taken off and been copied.

But has it all been worth it? As the merry-go-round has grown more and more frenetic, retailing has become increasingly dominated by the notion of change for change's sake. The public has revelled in the novelty of the new, and competition has bred better products and more relaxed and convenient stores. However, there are signs that some of this orgy of spending by the retail companies is beginning to produce diminishing returns. Lower-than-expected profits from some of the retailers in 1986 and 1987 suggested that perhaps the novelty was wearing off.

In this non-stop search for innovation it has been all too easy to write off the high street as doomed to be a casualty of progress, a half-way house between the medieval street market and the computerised, sanitised, super-discount megastore. On the face of it, the high street does indeed seem illogical. The car might as well not have been invented, for the amount of parking available. And when you get there you are expected to trudge around with a growing burden of shopping until you can take no more and stagger to a bus queue or fight for a taxi.

But in the name of comparison shopping, the high street still achieves something that is not fully possible elsewhere. It allows the shops full rein to entice the public to think spending and persuade them to empty their pockets as often and as impulsively as possible – or even better, sign to prove that they are the rightful owners of a piece of plastic.

On the whole, spending is good for us. It keeps other people in work, and gives them the wherewithal to buy goods and services that keep us in work or in dividends from the companies that sell those goods and services. But individual retailers are not particularly concerned about the common good. They want you to spend with them, not the competitor next door. To accomplish that, they have to resort to variations on the stratagems and devices made holy by the fairground huckster. Whether you are genuinely intent on comparison shopping, examining value against value, price against price, or simply out for a stroll in the sun, the retailer's aim is to distract you for long enough to make you want to buy. The reasons are unimportant, as long as you spend.

The prudent retailer will not want you to overspend, or to buy something you are not sure about, because if you consistently overspend your precious piece of plastic may be taken away from you and if you do not like what you have bought you may not go back to his shop. Mind you, many a retailer is not that prudent: he would prefer you to spend now and ask questions later. If he is really good at window displays and snazzy advertising, he may even persuade you to forget about a previous unhappy experience.

Nevertheless, shopping has become much more a game of cat and mouse than ever before. Ian MacLaurin of Tesco has called it the quiet revolution. He told a conference in Vienna in 1986: 'All the available evidence indicates that advanced economies like those of the United Kingdom are entering a period of profound change. Arguably, Britain could now be regarded as the testing ground for the shape of economies to come; a model for the post-industrial future. For those concerned, it is a traumatic experience in which initiative is once again at a premium. This is 'The Quiet Revolution' that has transformed the retail industry in no more than forty years – and it continues, at accelerating pace. Indeed, the industry's problem today is no longer one of adapting to, or even initiating change, but of anticipating change itself.'

MacLaurin is a long way from the pre-war image of the bloated capitalist in pinstripe and spats, grinding the faces of the poor to pay for his next cigar. He knows that the game has changed, and he is not alone. Wise and shrewd businessmen, both retailers and manufacturers, recognise the primacy of the consumer today and know that they ignore his or her whims at their peril.

It is an inconvenient fact of life for those who seek to make money out of the public that the whim factories have been in full production lately. There has been more concentration on packaging than on product. In some areas, like electrical goods, really new products are still popping off the production lines at an impressive rate. But when it comes to the basics, like food and clothing, they have been reinventing the wheel for a long time now. All that has changed is the design and wrapping.

Design has genuinely improved some of the goods themselves, but nowadays the retail chain has become the product every bit as much as the goods it sells. A strange new language has crept into those parts of the high street that aspire to break new ground. Like newspapers, now shops have stories to tell, statements to make, occasionally a message to impart, all in an effort to make the goods more likely to move off the shelves.

And then there are the department stores, retailing's equivalent of Disneyland. Frumpy and unloved for so long, all of a sudden they are being turned into shopping experiences again, for that is what they were originally intended to be. They are being laid out more scientifically, yet on similar lines to supermarkets. To get to the everyday goods you have to pass through the accessories and the luxuries, while the real treats are there to tempt shoppers on their way out. In supermarkets the treats are the sweets at the checkout. The department store equivalents are the perfume counters by the main door.

But the biggest headache for any department store is an inevitable result of being on several floors: how to get the customer to go upstairs. Sir Ralph Halpern managed to take over Debenhams with the promise that its stores would be turned into galleria, where escalators would take the public up the centre well of the building so that they could be dazzled by the array of departments beckoning to them on every side as they ascended.

Like so many retailing ideas, galleria were first thought of in Britain but then developed in the United States. The turn-of-the-century equivalent of the escalator was the wide, sweeping staircase. More space, cheaper property and a broader imagination transmuted that into a grander version in America. Now it is returning.

Supermarkets, too, are a US refinement born out of the English street market. Instead of a host of individual traders shouting their wares, the Americans had the idea of one trader taking a large area and selling a wide range of goods which he could arrange to his best advantage. That also gave the trader bigger buying power to negotiate with the manufacturers and wholesalers.

Britain has also copied the American concept of the shopping centre, or mall, along with franchise chains, convenience stores and fast food. Even Marks & Spencers owes a debt to the Americans. Yet British retailers, like British broadcasters, continue to insist that they are the best in the world. The reason for this extravagant claim by the retailers is that they have so much less space to play with than their more expensive American counterparts, so controls have to be tighter and more efficient. The Americans do not have to contend with planning laws, which can make it frustratingly hard to launch a new retail chain on the edge of town, as Sainsbury and BhS have found with SavaCentre. However, for those shopkeepers who do win the approval of the authorities, the planners then become their guardian angels, protecting them from any direct rival opening up a hundred yards along the road.

And while the British pride themselves on their efficiency, they forget how superb the Americans can be at training staff. The bugbear of every big British shops chain is the salesperson who is either surly or standoffish. The US stores teach their staff to make contact, to say hello, to start a conversation of some sort. The bonhomie may be false, but it is a lot better than the nakedly pushy British sales assistant, often found prowling women's dress shops. Perhaps that is why the British are confident they are better at supermarkets: human contact is kept to a minimum.

Opinions vary about the taste of the food in McDonald's hamburger stores, as they like to call them, but no one can quibble about their sheer efficiency and their ability to motivate staff to do what are inevitably menial tasks. After more than a dozen years in Britain, McDonald's is only now cautiously beginning to sell franchises for independent caterers to run its outlets, even though franchising is its basic policy in the US.

The history of franchising in the UK is mottled with failures. Kentucky Fried Chicken had to crack down on its franchisees a few years ago because of slipping standards, and others have had their problems.

One of the most successful retail franchises is Body Shop, the chain which sells health care products. It is run by Anita Roddick, who is adamant that franchising works only if it is being used to expand an already successful business.

She explained: 'You have to control the spirit, the soul, of the company, with a spirit that borders on the manic. It's a

185

generic language. We say "that's not Body Shop, Body Shop wouldn't do that, she is or isn't a Body Shop girl". We are marketing a corporate smell, we are marketing theatre. My shops are colourful sweet shops, playgrounds that say "come and try". I want to preserve that. Franchisees are given a building pack which we control. We have strong area management, and we want to see their training plans. It all stems from a strong core to the business. The franchisees don't have to worry about products or ideas. What they have to worry about is knowledge of their staff and customer care. It's not a machine for turning out profits.'

Several of the people interviewed for this book recalled the motto that 'retail is detail'. Roddick, Sir Terence Conran and Stanley Kalms at Dixons are among those who are acutely aware that customers can be put off by the slightest thing, often something they are not conscious of.

That message has not been lost on Guinness, which has owned Lavells newsagents and Drummonds the chemists for some years, and in 1982 took a decision to make retailing one of its major divisions. It bought Martins the Newsagent, the tobacconists Lewis Meeson, R.S. McColl in Scotland and the UK licence for the 7-Eleven American convenience store chain. However, it became a casualty of the Guinness boardroom row when in 1987 Anthony Tennant, the new Chief Executive, decided to put the retailing operations up for sale as part of a reorganisation of the group.

In 1986 Brian Baldock, managing director of Guinness Development, was explaining: 'We have gone for a fragmented and not too well managed area of retailing, to which we could bring added value, modifying the offering. The thing that has aided us is that we have done a fantastic amount of research into psychological trends and lifestyle. That has given us a good edge in understanding the sort of brands we should come forward with. Our retail portfolio has been built through opportunity. The magic figure we went for was 1,000 outlets. Then you have the buying power to exert pressure on manufacturers and get advertising support. We saw that no one was doing convenience very well. Seven-Eleven offered the chance to go in for different hours of trading and a different product mix. We shall sell fresh food, and alcohol where we can obtain licences. We want to get more people into the branches, and get them to spend more when they are in there. But there is a staff problem: how do you get them tuned into professional marketing? You need people who are motivated enough to do that.'

Guinness' attention to detail went one step further than that. It had developed its own computer model to target likely newspaper demand. It analysed the local demographic mix, and combined that with readership surveys to show what the catchment area for each newsagent should be wanting to buy. It was tremendously successful, according to Baldock, so much so that the company had planned to turn the system on to confectionery and eventually sell it as a service to newspapers and other retail suppliers.

Along with attention to detail, the best retailers must know and practise the art of keeping everything simple and presenting it effectively. Every other retailing group pays homage to Marks & Spencer in this respect. In what amounted to a straw poll of the top two dozen firms, there is no doubt that M & S is the retailer's retailer, the one they all fear and would love to emulate. Even the banks, who are slowly starting to see themselves as retailers, take M & S as their yardstick for how it should be done. They also share the fear of M & S, which has been talking for some time about offering financial services and in 1987 was actually granted a Bank of England licence to take deposits. Many of its in-store Chargecard holders keep surpluses in their accounts because of the refunds they receive on returned garments. It is now a bank in all but name.

Money has become a key component of the retail revolution. The banks realise that they have to market their services more aggressively, in the all-important tactic of recruiting new account holders before their rivals capture them. They are moving not a moment too soon: non-financial retailers have been eyeing the banks as a potentially vulnerable high-street target, and have become irked by the amount of money the banks cream off in commission for allowing other retailers to accept Access and Visa credit cards.

The first reaction has been a rush by orthodox retailers to launch their own in-store cards. Research has shown that card-holders spend up to six times as much as they would if they were armed with cash or cheque books. And, in a curious way that has not been properly analysed, shoppers seem to feel more inclined to spend if they have an in-store card rather than a bank credit card, despite the fact that the in-store cards normally charge far higher rates of interest on unpaid bills. Nothing has caused more pain and anguish in the retailing revolution than plastic cards, because of the apparently irresistible temptation they represent. They are a direct result of the increased competition on the high street, designed to overcome the last inhibition to buy: can I afford it?

Retailers have been criticised for making cards so easily available. In their eagerness to clinch a sale, some shops have issued cards on the flimsiest of information about the applicant, relying on most people's sense of responsibility and hatred of getting into debt – or, at least, into too much of it.

The stores' interest charges partly reflect the additional overheads involved. But they are also a form of insurance policy for the store. If they can charge everyone a stiff rate of interest, an annual percentage rate of as much as 37 per cent in some cases, then that will help to make up for a higher incidence of non-payers. A growing number of households are being scarred by one spouse or another secretly trying to pay off a credit card bill that got out of hand. Some people are being driven into the hands of loan sharks as they desperately try to borrow from Peter to pay Paul.

Although the law is strict about who is allowed to take deposits from the public, it is nowhere near as tight in controlling those who lend. The reason is that lenders are using their own money at their own risk, but of course they also have the money to pursue debtors through the courts. If people really cannot trust themselves to control their impulses when they walk into a shop, then Parliament may have to step in. And that would bring the retail revolution to a crashing halt.

Retailing has undergone a status change in the past twenty years. The most notable impact has been on the quality of people willing to make a career of it. At one time few graduates would have considered working for a shops group, with the possible exceptions of Marks & Spencer or John Lewis. Now the industry is littered with graduates, lured by the upsurge in salaries in an area of high unemployment. Retailing has been the place to be, and those brighter minds have climbed high enough up the career ladder to sharpen the quality of management.

In the late 1980s consumers are also better educated. They have more money, less time and they are more cynical. They are starting to believe that they can effect change. They want sympathy with the product, and they want information and education. Design has brightened up the high street, but by comparison it can only be a cosmetic. No one chooses an airline by its livery, but by its safety record and its standard of service. And people only come into a shop once because of the design: they don't go back if the service or the products are no good.

That certainly seems to be the message of the retail revolution. Those in work do have more money to spend, but the vast majority are not going to bankrupt themselves just because a shop has revamped its nameplate. If they do decide to spend more in one shop, for whatever reason, then they are likely to spend less in another. That is what competition is all about. No retailer can afford to be too far out of step, as even Marks & Spencer discovered when the new clothes chains began making inroads a few years ago.

In the end, the consumer pays for all he or she sees, and that includes the shop itself. Retailers are nothing if not obliging, but they will only offer what the public is willing to pay for, deliberately or not. If the public tires of designer high streets, they will be abandoned as quickly as yesterday's bread wrapper. Many shoppers might regret that. The important point is that they should know what they are paying for.

But while living standards continue to outstrip the ability of technology to dream up new products in most areas, the extra spending power will be diverted by the retailers into competing with one another to provide glamour and interest, to excite curiosity. Retailing has become a branch of entertainment, even showbiz, and there is enough competition in most parts of the high street to ensure that the consumer does not quite pay through the nose for the razzmatazz.

Toys R Us and some of the other out-of-town operations have shown that there may be scope for the retailer offering the very opposite: a stripped-down shed with the biggest range of goods at the lowest prices, shorn of atmosphere. That is why the vogue for out-of-town shopping must be seen in context. It is largely a consequence of the all-pervasive car, which makes certain types of shopping more convenient. The lower property prices in greenfield sites also help to make retailing out there more competitive. But it is not going to replace the high street. It is simply another type of retailing service, and one which the planning authorities could stamp on at any stage. Retail parks have not been in existence long enough to judge their long-term effects. If, as some fear, they do turn surrounding high streets into wastelands, their life could be as limited as the now-derided tower blocks of flats.

Both high streets and out-of-town centres may in any case be radically reshaped by the advent of electronically-driven home shopping to cater for an ageing and more affluent population. The razzmatazz could go into seductive video presentations instead of big sheds or pretty shops. The computer is capable of programming regular details like a credit card number and regular purchases, leaving the consumer free to be diverted by that week's special offer.

But first the retailers will have to develop efficient delivery systems which can bring the goods to the customer's door when the customer wants them – in the evening, at weekends, and at specified times. The next retail revolution is likely to involve a revolution in standards of service, and that is something that sticks in the craw of many British workers.

'The British conception of retailing as buying and selling is denigrated, as something not quite proper,' Anita Roddick pointed out. 'The problem it has had is that people have always associated retailing with the shopgirl, or an assistant, something menial. It's all to do with the language we use. The other problem is that there are many charlatans in the industry, who do not value human potential and human labour. I believe that by the end of the century America will be the world's granary, Asia will be the workshop and Europe will be the playground, which means service, which means retailing. Unless we understand this we will be left behind.' The next decade will determine if she is right.

References

All Our Working Lives, by Peter Pagnamenta and Richard Overy (British Broadcasting Corporation 1984)

A Pedlar's Legacy, the origins and history of Empire Stores, by Patrick Beaver (Henry Melland, 1981)

Don't Ask the Price, the memoirs of the president of Marks & Spencer, by Marcus Sieff (Weidenfeld & Nicolson, 1987)

First With The News, the history of W.H. Smith 1792-1972, by Charles Wilson (Jonathan Cape, 1985)

John Spedan Lewis, edited by Hugh Macpherson (John Lewis Partnership, 1985)

Marks & Spencer, an anatomy of Britain's most efficiently managed company, by Dr K.K. Tse (Pergamon Press, 1985)

Pile It High, Sell It Cheap, the authorised biography of Sir John Cohen, by Maurice Corina (Weidenfeld & Nicolson 1971, reprinted 1978)

The Day The Pigs Refused To Be Driven To Market, by Robin Wight (Hart-Davis, MacGibbon 1972)

Index